# In the
# EYE
## of an
# EAGLE

## JOHN HENRY HARDY

# FOREWORD

Thanks to the outcome of the 2016 election and the duly elected Republican president, Donald J. Trump, the US economy began booming and the stock market began hitting historical highs, and a southern border wall was being built to check the influx of tens of millions of illegal aliens, many of whom were rife with diseases that had nearly been eradicated in the United States.

* * *

Members of the Chinese Communist Party, however, were incensed by the president's imposition of tariffs to quell the horrific trade imbalance between the US and China. The Chinese had been deliberately manipulating their currency, the yuan, for decades, which gave them an unfair advantage in the World Trade Organization (WTO), enabling them to dump cheap products on the world market and forced foreign companies to surrender their intellectual property in exchange for doing business in their country.

As the US tariffs imposed a strain on the Chinese economy, the world was suddenly plagued by an extremely contagious pandemic with the namesake Wuhan, the Chinese city where it originated. That locality had several virology labs that were funded by the World Health Organization, including multi-million-dollar grants from American taxpayers. Those labs were supposedly seeking cures for a variety of viruses. Allegedly, many individuals and many national governments came to believe they were really germ warfare labs and that the Wuhan virus was unleashed upon the world in revenge for the faltering Chinese economy.

The Chinese government knew of the virus outbreak but did not impose international travel restrictions to or from their country. However, it did lock down domestic travel to and from Wuhan. But the outbreak was not disclosed to the world for several months and soon the pandemic spread to every continent on Earth, and the Chinese doctor who alerted the world to its danger mysteriously disappeared.

* * *

The questions now are: Did the Chinese Communist Party deliberately initiate a viral terrorist attack on the free world to get even for their tanking economy by not curbing international travel to and from Wuhan after they learned of the outbreak? How far will the Chinese Communist Party go—or how far did they go—as they strive to dominate the world financially and militarily by any means possible with the intent of becoming the world's sole superpower much as Nazi Germany once tried to do?

* * *

Why is the left trying to change America's two-party political system to a one-party country that heretofore was a universal icon of freedom and liberty?

And why are the democrats supporting China's fictional stance about the outbreak and origin of the pandemic, and curtailing the passage of legislation designed to rekindle our once-prosperous economy to help relieve the suffering of untold millions of American citizens? They committed these atrocities to restore their waning political power, and because of their hatred of President Trump!

In response to the president's "Make America Great Again" campaign, the left-leaning democrats were willing to instigate the start of a Second American Civil War in order to foster their alleged goal of being the one absolute power via a one-party political system. Their goal of having millions of illegal aliens register with their party by maintaining an open borders policy would ensure the success of that endeavor.

They therefore instigated a series of uprisings across the nation that caused many sanctuary cities to lie in partial ruin and destroyed the iconic statues of America's colorful history. Allegedly, they intend to install an American political system that mimics the socialist governments that rule China, Russia, Vietnam, Iran, Venezuela, and Cuba, even though they are aware that historically no socialist government has ever survived the ages.

This tale, *In the Eye of an Eagle*, depicts what could possibly happen to an average American family and the entire

United States if the leaders of the Democratic Party succeed in their alleged coup to overthrow our duly elected president, change our democracy to a socialist government, and conspire to shred our Constitution in order to attain absolute and unprecedented political power.

# CHAPTER 1

The nation was delighted as four million new jobs were created when President Trumpmeyer removed thousands of environmental restrictions placed on American businesses and negated the penalty President Ogama imposed on citizens for not having health care insurance. Subsequently, unemployment rates for minorities, women, youths, and veterans fell to all-time lows, and four million people were lifted off food stamps. The president was also initiating new international trade agreements with China, South Korea, Canada, Mexico, India, and the European Union, creating more new jobs in America and easing the neatly one-trillion-dollar annual monetary hemorrhage wrought by the unfair trade practices of those nations.

However, the democrats refused to fund a border wall designed to keep out drug smugglers, human traffickers, MS-13 gang members, murderers, rapists, and a plethora of other criminals fleeing justice in their home countries. The wall would also help reduce the several-hundred-billion-dollar yearly tax burden spent for supporting the illegal aliens.

By rescinding restrictions placed on the military by the previous administration, the terrorist group, the Islamic State of Iraq and Syria (ISIS), had been destroyed in the Middle

East, and the American armed forces were again the strongest in the world, keeping our citizens and other nations safe from foreign and homegrown terrorists.

Then President Trumpmeyer fostered the largest tax cuts and financial reforms in American history, causing domestic retail sales to soar, and he also intensified the war against the opioid drug cartels, shrinking the number of rampant addicts and their deaths in the United States. This is just a partial list of the Trumpmeyer administration's achievements since he was sworn in after the 2016 election.

* * *

The 2020 Election Day is nearing, and Jose Feliz, an elderly holdover from the Ogama administration, is serving on the White House staff of the Domestic Policy Council. He knows there is only one way his party can defeat the president, and he silently stands by intently watching President Trumpmeyer scan through the council's annual report in the Oval Office.

Then the naturalized American citizen silently stepped backwards until he was standing directly behind the president, who was seated at the Resolute desk. Then slipping a dagger from inside his suit jacket he raised it above his head for the briefest of moments, angrily shouting "Allahu Akbar" before plunging the blade into the back of Ronald J. Trumpmeyer, the 45th duly elected President of the United States!

* * *

In the interval, Vice President Mike Fence is now leading the nation since it was obvious President Trumpmeyer wouldn't be able to assume his duties any time soon. Not surprisingly, Bo Viden, the democratic presidential nominee, couldn't stand the pace and his dementia had worsened considerably, which forced him to drop out of the race, and the runner-up, Vernie Flanders, was still recovering from another heart attack.

Into this void stepped Luther Garcia, who once claimed to be a conservative but was now an avowed socialist. He resigned his ambassadorship to the United Nations to throw his hat into the presidential race. It was too late for the current VP, Mike Fence, to organize his own presidential platform, and with the help of the illegal alien voting bloc, the shocked, fickle, and misinformed American electorate voted in the first socialist candidate as the 46th President of the United States.

* * *

Luther Garcia, a socialist, was elected President of the United States since former President Trumpmeyer was still in the hospital recovering from his near brush with death just weeks before the 2020 Election Day, November 3rd.

A holdover from the prior administration had stabbed the president in the back much to the delight of the Democratic Party, illegal aliens and their families, Antifa, the BLM radicals, the Boogaloo Bois, drug smugglers, the drug cartel heads, human traffickers, MS-13 gang members, Islamic fundamentalists, and the Chinese Communist Party. The border had been closed due to the COVID-19 virus, but the president's near demise caused masses of illegal aliens to once again swarm towards the southern American border in unprecedented numbers.

The newly elected socialist president had reopened the border and every detention center had been shut down due to the massive waves of undocumented aliens rushing through the ports of entry. After being coached by socialist lawyers, the invaders began bringing children with them, who were not their biological offspring, and claiming refuge from alleged persecution in their native lands or seeking a better life in the land of the free. This new wave of undocumented aliens was overrunning the country, and millions were being released into the local communities by the ultra-liberal Ninth Circuit Court to await a hearing as to whether or not they were eligible for citizenship.

There were so many hundreds of thousands of them that the courts were overwhelmed, and Border Patrol agents were required to issue them citations ordering them to appear before an immigration judge on a scheduled date for a hearing. However, after they were released into society, most of the immigrants soon disappeared into the interior of the country and would never appear before the court. No arrest warrants were issued for them despite the fact they had broken a federal law.

This occurred because the present and past members of Congress, fearful of endangering their reelection bids and the wealth their power personifies, refused to address the gaping loopholes in America's immigration laws.

* * *

The Tri-Party now dominating American politics became the new face of the old Democratic Party, which was rapidly fading into history. It was formed from the splintered factions of the old party when Socialists, Progressives, and Liberals in the House relegated the Speaker, Mandy Melosi, to a mere figurehead, and soon even the few democratic die-hard moderates followed suit and pledged their allegiance to the new party and its goals.

The new lax election laws in the sanctuary states allowed all undocumented aliens to vote in local and state elections, and their ballots could sway two thirds of the state legislatures to convene an Article V Convention with the intent of changing America from a constitutional republic to a socialist nation—a communist nation.

* * *

"I say again," Nathan Bainbridge, a Tri-Party senator from California and one of the most senior and powerful men in the senate, ranted, "we will soon be tearing down this border wall constructed by the evil Trumpmeyer administration. It has been preventing our global brethren from receiving the love and support of the people of California and many other sanctuary states.

"Our former governor, Jerry Greene, had declared California a sanctuary state, and Governor Gavel Oldsome continues the quest of welcoming one and all to this safe haven.

"I have introduced Senate bill S401 that when ratified by the Congress will fully empower the states to determine who can legally vote in our federal elections, and also ensure that our international borders will forever remain open."

Even though most of the crowd wore COVID-19 masks, he could clearly hear the cheers and when they subsided he said, "I fully support the state law that makes certain that every Californian, including our undocumented aliens, receives

Medi-Cal benefits until the pending congressional Medicare for All bill is passed and signed into law by the president."

Again, he waited until the raucous cheering ended before continuing, "I am also calling upon the all 50 state legislatures to convene an Article V Convention to amend the Constitution to make any type of barriers on our southern and northern borders unconstitutional, and to modify the Second Amendment to make the possession of any type of firearm a felony for private citizens; only the police and the military will be armed. Therefore, any private citizen currently owning a weapon would be required to turn it over to any law enforcement agency under penalty of the law." There was another rousing cheer from the partisan crowd!

"Bill S401 will also make a naval blockade of our east and west coasts illegal if the purpose is to prevent any undocumented aliens from entering our country by sea. Once these federal laws are passed, then we'll be able to tear down this immoral wall that was built by that criminal Ronald J. Trumpmeyer!"

A roar of approval again emanated from the throats of thousands of Tri-Party supporters, and despite the masks their cheers echoed across the landscape. When the crescendo began to lull, the senator continued speaking, "Believe me when I say ..."

* * *

Six hundred yards away from the San Ysidro Port of Entry, where Senator Bainbridge was speaking and pointing toward the Mexican border, an amber-eyed Eagle was peering through the Scout Sniper daytime scope on his M16A4 rifle.

*OK you Tri-Party bastards,* he thought, *your ilk started this war by attempting to kill our duly elected president!* Then he pulled back the bolt and chambered a 5.56mm NATO round.

The sniper, an American Eagle, was one of millions of patriots determined to keep the United States from falling into the clutches of an eternal president—a virtual dictatorship that the Tri-Party was now advocating. The Eagle knew that was the ultimate goal of the Socialists, Progressives, and Liberals that had taken undisputed control of the old Democratic Party.

The senator turned his head as he continued lashing out at former president Ronald J. Trumpmeyer, and although the Eagle couldn't hear the senator's vitriol, his political views were well known. *This one is for you, Mr. President,* the Eagle thought, as a string of familiar commands began flowing through his psyche; *tighten your grip, center the reticle, wait for the kick.* As soon as the sniper saw the senator fall, he abandoned the desert spider hole where he had been concealed for several days and faded into the Sonoran Desert as silently as the shot he fired.

* * *

The news flashed across the TV screens and newspapers of every major media outlet around the world, and FBI agents swarmed over the San Ysidro Port of Entry. Except for the attempted murder of former President Ronald J. Trumpmeyer, Senator Bainbridge was the first nationally-known victim of the undeclared Second American Civil War that had allegedly begun as a result of the 2016 election results, which the left refused to accept!

* * *

The bullet had damaged the senator's head so badly that forensics couldn't immediately determine from which direction the projectile had been fired, and not one person from amongst the thousands attending the rally heard the fatal shot. The San Diego medical examiner soon identified the bullet as a 5.56mm slug.

"Whoever the killer or killers are," Dr. Calvin Ray, the San Diego ME said, "they are obviously an expert shot. There was no exit wound. The bullet impacted the victim's forehead and tore through his soft brain tissue before lodging against the back of his cranium."

He held the bullet up between his thumb and index finger so FBI Agent Alan B. Johnson could see it and then continued, "As you know, the 5.56mm slug is the standard military issue for the American M16 Rifle, and judging from the condition of the round, it traveled a great distance before hitting its target. It flattened out as it penetrated his skull, causing severe brain damage. The shooter or shooters may have a military background."

"That's what I was thinking," the FBI agent replied.

"There were no drugs or alcohol in the senator's blood," the doc added as he looked down at the cadaver lying on the gurney, "and my autopsy revealed he was in relatively good health for his age."

* * *

The FBI, San Diego's CSI team, and other forensic techs scoured the immediate area and the surrounding desert for more than a month. They knocked on hundreds of doors in the Chula Vista community and in Imperial Beach south of San Diego, but no one heard or saw a thing. The searchers passed by the camouflaged trap door covering the sniper's hide on several occasions, but they didn't discover the cleverly-hidden spider hole. Neither the weapon nor the ejected shell casing was ever found.

FBI Agent Alan B. Johnson and his team also scrutinized every multi-storied building in San Ysidro and Ocean View Hills proper, even though his team knew the distance from the nearest buildings in those cities to the San Ysidro Port of Entry was far beyond the maximum effective range of an M16 rifle, hoping someone saw or heard something suspicious that might eventually pinpoint the spot from where the shooter had fired the fatal shot.

Then his team got permission from the Mexican government to venture into Tijuana; still there was no break in the case. They went so far as to obtain satellite photos of the boats and yachts that were in the Gulf of Santa Catalina at the time of the shooting, hoping to spot something suspicious, but nothing panned out. The surveillance tapes of travelers entering and exiting the airports in San Diego, Los Angeles, Brown Field Municipal Airport, and Phoenix Sky Harbor didn't reveal any persons of interest entering or exiting the facilities in the days prior to the killing, and no known criminals or suspicious individuals were identified in the lines at the ticket counters. It was extremely frustrating. The FBI couldn't come up with a single clue!

The government utilized the news media too and offered a million-dollar reward for any information leading to the arrest and conviction of the killer or killers of Senator Bainbridge. The public called in thousands of tips and offered a multitude of hypothetical situations, but they all turned out to be dead ends. It seemed as though the sniper had disappeared into thin air, and the alacrity and ability of every law enforcement agency involved in the case soon came under intense public scrutiny. It was also a confounding and exhausting situation for the newly elected president, the Central Intelligence Agency, and the National Security Agency, but the investigation continued unrelentingly by every investigative body at every level of the federal and local governments.

* * *

The Socialists, Progressives, and Liberals that composed the newly-formed Tri-Party had seized control of the presidency and the House of Representatives, but not the Senate or the Supreme Court. They lionized Senator Bainbridge and pointed fingers at their republican counterparts, accusing them of a murder-for-hire plot. Their allegations angered republicans, and the legislation Senator Bainbridge sponsored, Bill S401, failed to pass muster in the Senate by a narrow margin of three votes. All across the nation, citizens were in an uproar. Along with the highly contagious Wuhan pandemic that didn't wane during the warmer months as expected, the government now had a mounting national uprising with which to contend.

The Supreme Court of the United States ruled that the portions of the border wall that had been erected by the Trumpmeyer administration would remain standing in spite of the socialist president's executive order, and the naval blockade of the American coasts enforced by the US Coast Guard and the US Navy to prevent the incursion of the illegal aliens from other continents would also continue. However, these were small and insignificant victories for the patriots in light of the recent Tri-Party political triumphs.

# CHAPTER 2

Sister Mary Theresa looked out at the raindrops splattering against the windowpanes of her modest room in the convent of Saint Hedwig's parish in New York City. Despite the overcast day, she could clearly see the cross on the church's spire from her third-story chamber. Another murder occurred in the neighborhood last night and the nun fervently prayed aloud, "May the Lord have mercy on his soul."

She had already said her morning prayers on her knees and was now heading toward the dining room where the other members of the Order of Saint Francis were assembling for breakfast. The Mother Superior, Sister Mary Clarinda, was already seated at the head table, and after she said grace the topic turned to the death of Pedro Rico.

"What a shame," the Mother Superior said, "that Mr. Rico never had a chance to say the Act of Contrition to beg God's forgiveness and cleanse his wretched soul before he died."

"Yes, Mother Superior," Sister Grace Pierre chimed in, "and I have one of his three children in my eighth-grade class. The family must be devastated."

"Detective McShane called me last night," the Mother Superior interjected, "and warned us to be very careful. The

New York City Police Department believes they are dealing with a sociopath, a serial killer, who hates the illegals and those who support them.

"'God only knows who his next victim will be,' he warned us because many of the Christian churches in the country are concealing, feeding, and sheltering the undocumented aliens as best as they can, and the Holy Father has given them his blessings, encouraging us to continue our humanitarian efforts in the name of the Lord."

After breakfast, the convent became as silent as a tomb. The teachers and the Mother Superior, who was also the principal at Saint Hedwig's school, headed toward the K through 12 building that was adjacent to the convent. The nuns, who were registered nurses and worked the 12-hour day shifts, took the subway to Saint Vincent's Hospital in Downtown Manhattan to relieve those who worked the prior tour. The remaining sisters waited for the parish bus that would drop them off at the numerous soup kitchens run by Catholic Charities. Their job was to feed the escalating numbers of illegal aliens as well as the burgeoning number of indigent American families. COVID-19 was again wreaking havoc on the economy, and millions of Americans and undocumented aliens were out of work again, so the soup kitchens were becoming a hallmark of every major metropolitan area in the United States.

Sister Ames, who was the cook, remained in the convent with her lay assistant, and they soon headed for the kitchen to begin preparing lunch and to plan the menu for dinner.

Sister Theresa was a novitiate and did not have a nursing or teaching degree and was therefore assigned duties as a housekeeper, and she quickly began collecting the breakfast dishes and doing other cleaning chores. The other members of the Order did not envy her assignment since it made for a long and lonely day.

* * *

Detective Mike McShane, a six foot two Irish American with short brown hair and blue eyes, came from a long line of law enforcement officials in the New York Police Department. His grandfather had been First Deputy Commissioner, and his father was a retired inspector. Mike was the leading investigator in the Pedro Rico murder case, and he knew the victim's record well.

Rico was an illegal alien and one of the most prolific drug dealers on the West Side. However, the NYPD could never obtain enough credible evidence to arrest him for any of his crimes, ranging from petty larceny to homicide. The mayor and the city council prohibited the NYPD from turning any illegal aliens over to the Immigration and Custom Enforcement officers for arrest and deportation much to the humiliation of the nation's largest police force.

Recently, Rico had been a person of interest in the murders of three lesser-known drug dealers, whose bodies were discovered within the fringes of his so-called "territory," and although Rico's friends had checkered backgrounds, they provided him with an airtight alibi, swearing he was playing cards with them at the time of the triple murders.

The NYPD was aware that Rico's associates were illegal aliens, addicts, and / or convicted felons—well-paid and trusted drug runners that kept the Rico gang well supplied with heroin, cocaine, fentanyl, ludes, and hashish. They were veteran criminals and knew the ins and outs of how to avoid detection and arrest. Mike McShane was certain Pedro Rico or his gang rubbed out the three drug pushers who were intruding on his territory but he couldn't prove it.

Detective McShane noted the victim was still donning an N-95 mask to prevent the spread of COVID-19, and that he was hit in the front of his forehead. There was no exit wound. The small amount of blood indicated he had died instantly, and several hundred dollars lay near his outstretched right arm. A search of his jacket and pants pockets produced 19 tiny plastic bags of heroin and ten one-hundred-dollar bills.

"Obviously," Mike said to the uniformed cops securing the crime scene, "the motive wasn't robbery. If a druggie or another dealer had killed him, they would have taken all the money and the drugs and then split."

The patrolmen agreed and Detective McShane continued, "Apparently, an addict was buying a fix when somebody blew Rico's head off, and the druggie probably ran off in fear of their own life. Let's hit on our snitches and find out why Rico himself was pushing the dope and not his gang members."

The uniformed officers scoured the immediate neighborhood in search of possible witnesses to the Rico killing. The murder had occurred on Tenth Avenue between West 48th and West 49th Street probably around eleven p.m., but nary a soul heard or saw anything. The detective was not surprised. The residents living in and around Hell's Kitchen would rarely, if ever, admit they saw or heard anything connected to a crime. It was the safest thing to do considering the crime syndicate's network of spies and strong-armed thugs.

After the medical examiner arrived and determined the cause of death was undoubtedly the gunshot wound, the photographer took numerous pictures of the crime scene, and the coroner's office soon whisked the body off to forensics. Detective McShane placed the money and the opioids into separate envelopes and headed to the police lab on Jamaica Avenue in Queens so the techs could access the database to get a name that matched any other prints on the money and to analyze the drug contents.

Mike and his team then called on their local snitches, but the only rumor was that the NYPD's recent crackdown on drug dealers throughout the five boroughs had caused many of Rico's known distributors to go underground, forcing him to do some of the leg work on the streets. However, the stoolpigeons could only describe the sniper as a rogue vigilante, an elusive shadow moving silently through the alleys and up the sides of buildings, jumping from rooftop to rooftop.

But no one could come up with a name or where he came from or when or why this mysterious figure was stalking the criminal elements plaguing the city. It was the third sniper killing of an illegal alien in New York within several weeks of Senator Bainbridge's death, and the murder rate by other means was on the rise in every major city across the United States although the public was unaware of it.

* * *

The bureau chief, Dan Fitzgerald, called Detective McShane on his cell phone and told him that the police commissioner requested his presence at One Police Plaza ASAP, and the concerned detective soon pressed the elevator button for the 14th floor. The commissioner's secretary, Angeline Blake, announced McShane's presence and ushered him into the inner sanctum of the PC's office.

To Mike's surprise, the newly elected mayor of the City of New York, Francisco Alvarez, was seated next to the commissioner's desk. His Tri-Party had seized the political power in this sanctuary city-and the liberal city council, with the prior mayor's prodding, had granted the illegal aliens the right to vote in local elections. Their numbers provided the mayor with a narrow margin of victory. Neither the mayor nor the PC acknowledged the detective's entrance. They were locked in a heated conversation about the Rico murder.

"This is the third murder of an undocumented alien this month," the red-faced mayor shrieked at the police commissioner, and asked "What the hell is the NYPD doing about it?"

"I've got our best investigator on the case, Mayor," Commissioner Hereford replied as he looked over at the detective. "This is Detective Michael McShane."

The mayor turned his head toward the detective and asked, "Well?"

"Well, Mayor," Detective McShane began, "we're comparing the slugs from the first two victims with the one that killed Mr. Rico, and I don't have any answers yet, but the lab report should be available soon." There was a long moment of silence.

"That's it?" the mayor angrily retorted as he glanced down at the document he was holding. "I've got forty thousand sworn officers on the payroll, driving nine thousand seven hundred patrol cars, riding forty five horses, and flying eight helicopters, and the only damned thing the NYPD can tell me is that this mysterious suspect might be a serial killer!" Then he looked back up at Mike.

"Well, Mayor," Detective McShane explained as he tried to keep his boss out of trouble, "we believe he is using a silencer, which explains why no one ever hears the shots. We have nothing on our surveillance cameras, no prints, and not one of the tips we received from the public is panning out. There are more than eight million five hundred thousand people in New York City and any one of them could be a suspect."

"I don't need some second-rate detective lecturing me on how many people live in New York City, McShane," the mayor shouted. "I damned well know how many citizens live here!"

"I'm sorry, Mayor," Mike started to say, "I didn't mean to imply . . ."

"My Public Affairs Office is being deluged with calls from those eight million plus citizens and undocumented aliens," the mayor kept on shouting without acknowledging the detective's apology, and turning his head back toward the police commissioner, he rambled on, "New Yorkers are too frightened to leave their homes and walk the streets. The situation has deteriorated so badly that the influx of aliens into the city has slowed despite the newly-opened border. During my campaign I promised New Yorkers that this city would retain its sanctuary status and we'd make everyone feel safe and welcome, and I intend to keep that promise."

"I understand that perfectly well, Mr. Mayor," the police commissioner replied, "and we will continue to do our best."

Robert Hereford was a hold-over from the previous administration that was composed of the old Democratic Party members, and he was less than two years into his five-year appointment as police commissioner, but he didn't want to retire under the present circumstances after having served the city for more than 30 years.

"Well *Mr. Commish*," the mayor sarcastically snapped as he accentuated the shortened title, "your best isn't good enough at this point. Just keep in mind that the police commissioner of the city of New York serves at the pleasure of the mayor."

"Yes Mayor, I am well aware of that," the commissioner replied. He felt a twinge of anxiety at the mayor's remark.

But the PC knew the mayor couldn't find an experienced socialist within the NYPD to immediately replace him, and the city council was scouring the country for a qualified candidate. Normally, the mayor's office would be deluged with a list of wannabe police commissioners, but there was a paucity of qualified applicants given the city's current chaotic state; New York was the epicenter of COVID-19 in the United States, and now violence was erupting between the two political factions all across the city, the Tri-Party and the Republican Party.

*When he finds a qualified applicant,* Robert Hereford thought, *I'll be forced to retire.*

The mayor noted the detective was more composed under his bombastic scrutiny than the police commissioner was, and he decided to test McShane's mettle even further.

"Tell me detective," he asked, "what exactly does the NYPD do for the people of New York, America, and the 11 foreign cities where our counter-terrorism teams operate?" His angry brown eyes glared into the steely blues of one of New York's finest, but the detective never blinked or flinched.

"Sir," Detective McShane countered as he leaned slightly forward, "The mission of the NYPD is to enforce the law, preserve peace, reduce fear, and provide for a safe environment."

The mayor was flabbergasted. The reply was so quick and so precise that for the first time since he took office, the mayor felt a slight twinge of confidence in the department for which he cared or knew precious little, and for a long moment the detective's blazing blues and the mayor's angry browns locked in a stare that seemed to indicate they were of equal rank.

"Well, the NYPD isn't accomplishing its mission," the mayor finally remarked. "I've got a news conference scheduled ten minutes from now in front of City Hall," he continued as his eyes finally turned back toward the police commissioner. "The Wall Street Journal, The New York Times, the

Daily News, and the New York Post—plus a dozen or so TV stations and their media reps—will be there. A slew of international reporters and those damned small-town conservative newspaper vultures are also chomping at the bit as well. They want to know what the hell the NYPD is doing to solve these killings. I'll introduce you commissioner, and then you can have Detective McShane explain to the media where we stand on this case at the moment."

"Yes, Mayor," the commissioner answered.

Detective McShane was dumbfounded! He had never appeared on national television! As they followed the mayor toward the door, Commissioner Hereford winked at Detective McShane to indicate he said the words the mayor needed to hear, and the threat he made concerning the PC's job security was meaningless—at least for now. However, the PC's gesture did little to quell the detective's anxiety about appearing on national television.

* * *

The Socialists, Progressives, and Liberals, along with the media and a plethora of undocumented aliens, had gathered on the steps at City Hall and loudly cheered as the mayor stepped before the rolling cameras and popping flashbulbs. The illegal aliens had been granted the right to vote in local elections, and their numbers jolted the mayor into office just as the city's left-leaning city council intended they would. It was an historic event as Mayor Alvarez was only the second Hispanic elected Mayor of New York City since John Purroy Mitchel was sworn in as the city's chief executive in 1913.

"Socialism has triumphed in New York City with my election," the mayor shouted to the partisan crowd, "and it will remain a sanctuary city as long as I am the mayor!" He waited until the raucous cheering abated before continuing his rhetoric.

"The country no longer has to live under the dictates of the evil Trumpmeyer administration!" he eagerly proclaimed, "But unfortunately, Jose Feliz didn't completely finish the job!"

Again he relished the resounding accolades and chants of what had become the Tri-Party's signature slogan, "No more Trumpmeyer, no more wall, no more USA at all." Those jeers from the crowd echoed down the canyons formed by the buildings lining Broadway, Park Row, and Chambers Street despite the COVID-19 masks most were wearing. The sound flowed to the ears of the American Eagle! He couldn't hear the partisan crowd's chanting clearly, but he knew that refrain always betrayed their jubilation at President's Trumpmeyer's near brush with death.

That was bad enough, but it was their delight in celebrating the demise of his country that incensed the Eagle most. He had defended America and other countries during his three tours in Iraq and Afghanistan, and he was not going to surrender his country to the Communist Party now or ever. He and millions like him would rather die!

Smiling, Mayor Alverez again listened to the roaring crowd with his arms raised above his head with the middle and index fingers of his hands spread and extended to form a V, the symbol of victory. He again waited for the rousing ovation to subside before he spoke again.

"Our new school curricula will be similar to the model instituted by the Los Angeles public school system," the mayor said, "where more than 20 foreign languages are spoken in the classrooms. Currently, most of the undocumented aliens in LA, 'Frisco, and New York came from a multitude of countries and speak only their native tongues. Many of these students are also the anchor babies of undocumented aliens and come from homes where English is not spoken.

"A shortage of qualified teachers and school supplies are wreaking havoc on the thousands of these students whose enrollments are challenging our educational system," the mayor finally continued, "and our paucity of medical clinics and a shortage of public housing is clogging our emergency rooms and forcing our newest citizens to live on the streets in cardboard shacks and tents made of canvas and blankets. These shortfalls will be addressed more fully during my administration; more English as second language teachers will be hired, more clinics will be opened, and the building of additional public housing will commence as soon as possible." Once again raucous cheering ensued from the partisan gathering.

"To pay for the additional services, I will cut into the over-bloated budgets of the New York Police Department, the fire department, sanitation, probation, Board of Corrections, transportation, and several other departments," the mayor declared. "The money saved by these cutbacks will be shifted to our social programs to feed, clothe, educate, and house our newest residents and to hire more instructors to teach them English."

Once again he smiled broadly and listened to the enthusiastic response of the narrow-minded crowd. "The upcoming winter would be devastating for many of our new brethren," he continued, "and I am urging New Yorkers to welcome these poor folks into the comfort of their homes during the severest weather, since all our public shelters are already overcrowded and building or acquiring additional public facilities will take time."

The native New Yorkers knew the city was already mirroring the plight of San Francisco and Los Angeles, and they were growing angrier by the day. Garbage and feces littered the once-clean sidewalks, streets, and gutters. After the garbage was picked up by the sanitation department, the streets, sidewalks, and gutters were hosed down, flushing the raw sewerage into the storm drains that poured into the East River, the Harlem River, and the Hudson River.

However, the mayor knew his intentions and edicts did not sit well with millions of native New Yorkers, but he didn't care since the Tri-Party was now in power. Many native citizens believed the election was rigged, but a recount proved Francisco Alvarez had won by a narrow margin thanks to the undocumented aliens living in the city, and therefore he was the duly elected mayor.

* * *

This was the first public appearance of the mayor since he won the recent election, and he did not want to be the bearer of bad news about the sniper. He would place that onus on Robert Hereford, the police commissioner, who was a holdover from the prior Democratic administration. In spite of this fact, the mayor considered him to be a political enemy, and as he introduced the PC to the crowd he made a comment about the unsolved case of the sniper killing the three undocumented aliens and a loud chorus of hissing and boos erupted from the partisan crowd.

Detective McShane noticed the mayor conveniently left out the fact there were many other murders in New York and other metropolitan areas across the country since the violence erupted, and the greatest number of victims were not illegal aliens, but American citizens of every color, race, and creed.

"Rest assured my fellow New Yorkers," the commissioner began, "the city is safe for the average citizen. The killer or killers are allegedly vigilantes, who are targeting criminals, such as the drug dealers, MS-13 gang members, human traffickers, and the rapist who had been terrorizing victims in the Central Park, East Side, and Yorkville districts. However, what he or she is doing is outright murder! Rest assured the NYPD is working day and night to solve these cases and to apprehend the killer."

His last remark was also greeted with jeers from the partisan crowd.

"Detective Michael McShane," the commissioner continued, "is leading the investigation, and he will now update the media and the citizens of New York on the progress we have made thus far. Detective?"

Detective McShane took a deep breath and anxiously stepped up to the mike. "The killer appears to be working alone," he began, "since the bullet that killed Mr. Rico matches the slugs taken from several other undocumented aliens who also have criminal records." The crowd hissed and booed at his last remark.

The detective swallowed hard and continued. "We are currently comparing the bullet that killed Mr. Rico with every other recent homicide in the city. However, this particular sniper is using a silencer and fires at his victims from a great distance, which leaves us with no solid clues and makes his apprehension impossible at this moment. We are asking the public to report any suspicious activity to the police—no matter how small or insignificant it seems to be . . ."

At that moment, almost 600 yards away on the fifth floor of a parking garage next to a high-rise office building, the Eagle's amber eye continued to peer through the Scout Sniper daytime scope. He could hardly hear the mayor's words over the loudspeaker system, but he heard the enthusiasm in the mayor's voice concerning the budget cuts and the responses of the jubilant crowd; he waited for the right moment.

As the detective was speaking, the Eagle continued peering through his variable SSDS and adjusted the intensity until his target was more clearly visible. When the mayor turned his head in the right direction, the Eagle centered the reticle on his forehead then gently squeezed the trigger, and a mere second later Mayor Francisco Alvarez fell face down on the steps of City Hall!

The police commissioner and the detective rushed down the steps, and the stunned crowd backed away from the mayor's prostrate form. Everyone thought the mayor had slipped and fallen, and the sudden glimmer of flash bulbs was almost blinding. The two men approached and then knelt down next to the mayor's prone figure, but they suddenly looked up and stared at one another for a long moment.

It was mortifying. There was no point in checking for a pulse. They could see the exit wound on the back of his skull. Detective McShane looked back up at the police commissioner, whose face was as white as a sheet. The newly elected mayor of the nation's largest city had just been murdered before the eyes of the world!

"We just got done announcing to the world that the sniper was targeting criminals only," the commissioner softly said, "and now this. Not only was he the mayor, but he was also a naturalized citizen—a Hispanic. We're really up to our ass in alligators now!"

* * *

Someone in the crowd suddenly screamed, "It's the sniper," and the frightened and frenzied crowd scattered down the steps like thistle down being blown about by a whirlwind, while others fled up the steps and into the safety of City Hall. Both the PC and the detective drew their Sig Sauer 9mm pistols and glanced up and down either side of the municipal building but didn't see anything suspicious. There were no more shots. Apparently, the mayor was the sole target.

The on-scene paramedics rushed to the fallen mayor, while a multitude of uniforms followed Detective McShane as he tore down the steps of City Hall toward Elk Street and Tweed Courthouse, with his pistol in one hand and his gold shield in the other, but no one there heard or saw anything suspicious.

The posse then ran all the way over to Chambers Street, but they saw nothing other than fellow New Yorkers going about their business. Then they dashed west to Broadway and scanned the multi-storied buildings across the way, but everything looked calm and peaceful.

Meanwhile, another group of uniformed police, led by a sergeant, ran to the back of City Hall to Steve Flanders Square and then fanned out and kept on moving all the way into City Hall Park and down to Jacob Wrey Mould Fountain, but they too came up empty-handed. No one roaming about City Hall Park saw or heard anything out of the ordinary.

The band then sprinted to the opposite side of the park and stopped at Center Street and then tore down to Park Row. They carefully scanned the area around the Ben Franklin Statue and Printing House Square, but all they saw were people heading for the businesses located there and the usual rush of street traffic. No one there was aware of the pandemonium and the terrified crowd on the other side of the street.

* * *

The Eagle remained hidden behind the row of parked cars that composed his hide, quickly broke down the M16 rifle, and removed his work clothes from the suitcase before stuffing the weapon and the spent cartridge into it. Then he quickly stripped down to his underwear and stuffed the blue business suit and accessories into the suitcase with the rifle before slipping into his everyday work apparel.

He cautiously observed the foot traffic casually walking to or from their cars, unaware of the tragedy at City Hall. The Eagle looked warily around to be certain no one noticed his departure, but the nearest New Yorkers were too far away to be of any concern. As the driver in the last car who was searching for a parking place slowly drove by, the Eagle nonchalantly stepped out from his hiding place, rode the elevator down to the ground floor, hailed a cab, and then coolly disappeared into the midmorning crowd. It was imperative he got back to work before he was missed.

* * *

By the time Mike arrived back at City Hall, the area had been sealed off and the horrified and curious crowd had reappeared but was being kept at a distance from the crime scene. Luckily, a forensic tech discovered the spent bullet lodged in the wooden door frame of City Hall. After he dug the slug out, he showed it to the police commissioner and the detective.

"It looks like a 5.56mm round," he mumbled to the PC and then looked at the pained expression on Mike McShane's face. He certainly did not envy their jobs at the moment.

The chief medical examiner, Dr. Simone Simpson, was examining the body. It was rather unusual that the chief ME, a three-star ranking officer in the NYPD, would be examining an on-scene murder victim, but she was at City Hall on business at the time of the shooting.

It is the ME's job to determine the manner and cause of death for people who die of criminal violence, and in this case it obviously was the bullet wound. There was no need to test his DNA. The cadaver had been positively identified as that of Francisco Alvarez, a member of the extreme left wing of the Tri-Party and the duly elected mayor of the City of New York. The news flash incited demonstrations around New York and other sanctuary cities across the United States; the Hispanic world was particularly incensed.

The mass news media was aware that the murders of less prominent citizens were happening daily across the country, but they failed to report them or that an alleged unconventional and undeclared civil war had stealthily begun erupting nationwide since the Tri-Party began playing a major contentious role in American politics and a Democratic hold-over had tried to assassinate former President Trumpmeyer.

To make matters worse in the Alverez case, the national news media reported that the American Civil Liberties Union and other activist groups threatened to sue, alleging that the PC was guilty of not providing sufficient police security to adequately protect the mayor. They avowed it was a classic case of dereliction of duty. They were also averring that the chief investigator, Detective Michael McShane, was dragging his feet in apprehending the sniper, because all the victims in New York thus far were undocumented Hispanic aliens except for the mayor. It was an outright lie, and yet all 50 left-leaning members of the New York City Council concurred with the ACLU's allegations.

* * *

Mike McShane was jolted out of his sleep and bolted upright. Sweat ran down his face and soaked into the collar of his white T-shirt. He took a few deep breaths and looked at the clock; it was three a.m., and he had been awakened by a nightmare, an image of the stalking, faceless sniper that had killed the mayor of the country's largest city, which made for national and international intrigue! Two weeks had passed since the mayor had been murdered, and the department still did not have a single clue as to the killer's identity. *The sniper is a very skilled and clever adversary,* the detective mused as he ran his fingers through his hair.

The deputy mayor, Phil Sandoval, had been sworn in as the new mayor, and had PC Hereford assign 100 detectives to the case. The only bright spot in this whole ordeal for Mike McShane was that he had been promoted to Detective First Grade, and during his celebration party the PC assured him he would be retained as the lead investigator in the sniper killings.

The image of the sniper quickly faded from his psyche, and Mike turned on the lamp on the nightstand on his side of the bed and stood up. He looked down at Gloria, his raven-haired wife. Even after having been married for more than 20 years and bearing a son and twin daughters she was still a beauty, and he was glad he hadn't awakened her.

They had been vacationing in Jamaica three years ago when she was bitten by a mosquito and became infected with the Zika virus, but her Guillain-Barre tests have been negative for the past three years. The GBS had been a total nightmare for him and the entire family. *Thank God she is cured,* he mused.

He sat on the edge of the bed for a few moments, but the sniper's faceless image returned and continually interrupted his reverie, and he knew if he laid back down his tossing and turning would eventually awaken his wife. He shut off the light and the alarm that was set for six a.m., strolled into the kitchen, and turned on the automatic coffee maker.

As he sat at the kitchen table waiting for the coffee to perk, his exhausted mind kept lulling him back to sleep, but each time he dozed off, an impulse of psychic energy intruded on his sleepy daze and caused his head to snap back up. With each nod, his thoughts kept drifting back to the nightmare and he repeatedly saw the ghostly figure again, but the last time he dozed off he saw the image of an iridescent number, a five, impinge on his psyche a split second before his eyes opened. It was an omen, but he didn't know what it meant and yet it fascinated him. *Perhaps,* he mused, *my prayers are summoning up a clue in my subconscious mind.*

The significance of the number kept taunting his curiosity, and while he sipped his morning brew he wrote down anything of significance in his life that involved the number five: his wife's birthday was May fifth; there were five brothers and sisters in his immediate family; he graduated fifth in his high school class; he graduated from the police academy on September fifth more than 20 years ago; and five months ago Senator Nathan Bainbridge was murdered in California. Mike shuttered at the thought, but then he slowly stood up and placed his half-empty cup down on the table. *The senator,* he mused, *was killed on December fifth at age 55 with a 5.56mm bullet!*

The intrigue now became so intense that he left his house at five thirty a.m. and headed for his Central Park Precinct office. Two hours later, he called the FBI's New York office and Agent Sara Glitz answered, and by eight a.m. Detective Mike McShane was on a flight out of LaGuardia, heading for the FBI's terrorist lab in Huntsville, Alabama.

Mike knew the FBI was still as clueless as the NYPD about the identity of the sniper. Lab tech Shelly Camatti was waiting for the detective when he arrived, and he handed her the envelope containing the bullet that killed Mayor Alvarez.

* * *

The escalating national turmoil forced the FBI, the NYPD, the CIA, and the NSA to make a significant and honest inquiry into why this peace-loving nation was now rife with violence. The conclusions they reached were not made known to the American public because they did not bode well for the newly elected president and most of the Congressional House members.

Before reading the report, however, Mike had sworn to the lab tech not to reveal the results of the FBI's report to anyone as it was extremely sensitive and brutally honest. It cast the left in an unfavorable political light and many leaders of the intelligence agencies who composed it would be fired if the socialist president ever got wind of the report.

The lab tech gave Mike McShane a copy to occupy his anxious mind as he sat in the waiting room of the Terrorism Lab waiting for the results of the bullet comparison test. The rather lengthy report concluded that, "These clashes between the socialists and conservatives began because the old Democratic Party refused to accept the results of the 2016 election and Trumpmeyer's wide lead in the polls during his 2020 reelection campaign. It was obvious the general public favored the conservative viewpoint, and this caused the spike in the animosity between the socialists and the conservatives that was now reaching a crescendo. The hostility continued and the furor sometimes became ultra-violent particularly when the Republican Party assembled and President Trumpmeyer had been the featured speaker.

"The crux of the problem between the conservatives and socialists," the report stated, "was the fact that the Republicans, the conservatives, claimed they are endeavoring to retain America's constitutional democracy, which is guaranteed by the Constitution. The left, however, wants to change the form of the American government to that of a Socialist regime.

"The right of the conservatives to assemble and achieve its goals was being threatened by the left-wing radical activists. Since the sanctuary city and state governments refused to protect the Republican demonstrators they are now forming paramilitaries, called American Eagle Militias, to protect their rights, just as the colonists did to protect their God-given rights that were desecrated by the British monarchy, and resulted in the outbreak of the American Revolutionary War.

"Among those conservative ranks are many middle aged and older Americans as well as many from the younger generation who do not share the anarchistic and socialistic values of Antifa, the Boogaloo Bois, and the BLM radical element that have become the enforcement arm of the Tri-Party," the report continued. "Many Republican military veterans permeated the conservative ranks and organized the militias into defense groups. Their main goal is allegedly to protect the conservatives who did not condone the radicalism of the left. They wanted to elect officials who are determined to retain our American way of life that had prospered for more than 244 years, thanks to a system that valued hard work and individual enthusiasm, which benefits the public, the worker, or an inventor."

"That economic system is known as capitalism," Mike McShane mumbled to himself, "and it is based on a free market system, which means the place of production and its subsequent products and their distribution is owned and operated by business corporations or individuals and not the federal government."

"On the socialist side," the report continued, "Antifa, the Boogaloo Bois, and the radical element of the BLM of the socialist Tri-Party consists of different age groups, but the majority is composed mostly of the younger generation, many of whom are millennials—the everything-for-free crowd.

"They were educated by the multitude of ultra-liberal college professors, whose life experiences are confined to a theoretical classroom environment, as opposed to a philosophical mixture of pragmatism and academic thinking that could foster a variety of productive applications in various fields of endeavor under capitalism.

"The arrogance of these college professors, wrought by grandiose feelings of intellectual superiority, fueled an 'everything-for-free attitude' and an anarchistic ego of self-importance that coincided with the Tri-Party's socialist views. Therefore, the conservative values of hard work, individual achievement, and capitalism are viewed with disdain, and conservative speakers have been permanently banned from college campuses across the country as a result.

"The Socialists vowed to forcibly change the United States into being a communistic nation by convening an Article V Convention to change the Constitution, since they believe capitalism exploits the working class. They want the government to control all the means of production of the goods and services produced in the United States, and to control the distribution of such merchandise and facilities. True to their Socialist ideology, they will do this by force if necessary.

"Antifa, a shortened term for anti-fascist, has been around for decades. They opposed Mussolini, Hitler, the Ku Klux Klan, white supremacists, and the neo-Nazis, especially in Germany. Their main objective is anarchy, the complete absence of government; they believe any kind of government unjustly interferes with individual liberty and should be replaced by the cooperative association of diverse groups, and if necessary, this must be accomplished by force. They claimed to be anti-racial, anti-sexist, and anti-homophobic. But they have always favored the left, and although they are still somewhat loosely organized, there are now factions springing up all across the US.

"Although some of Antifa's initial aims were honorable, their behavior in the United States radically changed with the results of the 2016 election, and their actions were now clearly anti-American, even though a Socialist had gained the presidency and they hold the majority in the House. Antifa's desire for anarchy, chaos, lawlessness, and their antigovernment bias puts them at odds with the socialist's viewpoint of one absolute party, and yet both factions have always favored the leftist viewpoint. However, this provisional axis between Antifa and the Socialists is a powerful synergism that could destroy the present form of our federal government and marginalize the entire 50 state governments.

"Then Antifa, the Boogaloo Bois, and the BLM radicals did the unthinkable. By force they seized a six square block of Seattle, Washington, and declared that section of the city an independent nation. They named it Chaz and drove out the police forces with the aid of their toady mayor, Jenny Durkan, who declared the coup to be an act of love; others viewed it as a festival. The idea soon began spreading to other cities in the sanctuary states.

"The enforcements arms ruled with an iron fist in Chaz and demanded free college, free food, no police force, no prisons, and universal recognition as an independent nation.

"At conservative events, Antifa thugs enjoy mimicking the sadistic killers of the Islamic Fundamentalist factions that were decapitating Christians in several parts of the world because of their faith. Antifa's imitation of symbolic decapitation was initiated by scowling and then running their index fingers across their throats and or briefly brandishing a knife; for many Americans it was a rather frightening ordeal. Terror and intimidation are part of Antifa's tactics if they do not win an election or a favorable ruling by one of their toady judges.

"The members of this radical group did not actually decapitate anyone thus far, but their threats, guns, knives, baseball bats, and beatings were effective in enforcing their dogma. Like the cowardly radical Islamic Fundamentalists and in typical fanatical fashion, those Antifa demonstrators hide their identity by covering their faces and heads with masks so only their eyes are visible.

"Unfortunately, this tactic coincided with the COVID-19 requirement of wearing masks to prevent the spread of the disease. But Antifa's intent was not medical safety. It is a tactic meant to thwart the facial identity technology available to law enforcement so as to remain anonymous to the police and the general American public during the news broadcasts of their demonstrations. Their far-left agenda and fanatical treatment of anyone who opposed the Tri-Party view forced former president, Ronald J. Trumpmeyer, to declare them a terrorist organization.

"The Black Lives Matter movement soon joined Antifa in the demonstrations. That organization was founded upon a report that a black man was shot and killed by police after he threw his hands up and surrendered. The Ogama administration's attorney general, Eric Folder, did an investigation and proved it was all a lie. However, it was a great excuse for BLM members to participate in the looting, beatings, intimidations, and extortion of local business owners under Antifa's control.

"Then another terrorist group has reared its ugly head. It is known as the Boogaloo Bois. Their main objective is the confrontation and destruction of the police force in any given state or city, thereby initiating the Second American Civil War, which they call the Boogaloo—an uprising that they believe will occur after the federal government tries to confiscate all firearms. They come to the protests armed with assault rifles, military fatigues, knapsacks, and wearing colorful Hawaiian luau shirts, which allude to the pigs roasted at the social gatherings in the 50th state. However, in this case it directly mimics the derogatory term pig that the Boogaloo Bois use to describe police officers.

"The Boogaloo Bois are far-right fanatics and use the term Boogaloo to refer to their anti-federal government attitude or their left-wing opponents. There are anti-government and anti-law enforcement groups, and some are white supremacy groups, who believe the uprising will be a race war. The groups primarily organize online, mostly on Facebook, and appear at anti-lockdown protests and the George Floyd protests.

"The uprisings plaguing the country were supposedly organized to protest the death of—and to seek justice for—George Floyd, who was murdered by a Minneapolis policeman. His killer was arrested and charged with murder. However, all the money collected by the Black Lives Matter movement during the fiasco that was allegedly protesting Mr. Floyd's death were being funneled into the Tri-Party coffers.

"The American Eagle Militias, on the other hand, are designed to counteract Antifa's and the Boogaloo Bois' threats at conservative political rallies, and the only common piece of apparel is a sea of red Make America Great Again hats that are a tribute to former president, Ronald J. Trumpmeyer. Their facial features are plainly visible, and their actions were in keeping with the constitutional right of all Americans to peaceably assemble; therefore, they did not interfere with the Tri-Party gatherings.

"In reaction to the leftist threats, the local American Eagle Militia commanders would telephone key members that in turn would notify the other adherents in the group. It was a quick and effective method to activate the militia members within minutes to protect the conservative supporters at any planned political rally or to protect prominent Republicans and their families from being intimidated at their homes, businesses, restaurants, or other public places.

"Their actions were essential since the mayors and governors in the sanctuary cities and states refuse to enforce law and order at conservative events as they were being harassed by the leftist radicals. This conservative reaction tactic worked well, particularly at the organized conservative rallies. However, the grave danger here is that both sides were now bearing arms, and if they exchanged gun fire at even one demonstration, an open and undeclared Second American Civil War might result."

* * *

Less than an hour later, Mike McShane had the answer. The bullet that killed Mayor Francisco Alvarez was fired from the same weapon that also killed Senator Nathan Bainbridge in San Ysidro, California! The FBI agent in charge of the terrorist lab was as stunned as the NYPD detective. It shed a whole new light on the case. The killer had murdered a senator, and that made it a federal case. But the rifle that killed Senator Bainbridge was also being used by a sniper that had traveled all the way across the country and murdered the mayor of a large sanctuary city. The killer had crossed state lines and thereafter Mike McShane knew the FBI would officially take over the Alvarez murder case and the other minority killings. It was obvious he would now be working closely with the FBI on the case in an attempt to bring the serial killer or killers to justice.

* * *

The FBI director and the NYPD commissioner did not want the public to know that Senator Bainbridge's murder and the New York City sniper cases were related. Thus, that part of the investigation had to be a covert operation. Its revelation would make it another national issue and intensify the turmoil raging between the Republican Party and the Tri-Party, since both sides were now openly accusing one another of the alleged murders, revenge shootings, beatings, and rapes that were on the rise in all 50 states as municipal police departments were being defunded and downsized, making the country a criminal's paradise.

Exposing the killings in the Bainbridge and Alverez cases to the general public might serve as another catalyst to deepen the hatred between the two major political parties, the FBI surmised, and could bring the struggle to a flash point, resulting in an open civil war, a conflict so endemic that not even the federal army would be able to contain it.

Thus far, however, the havoc wrought by gangs of socialist thugs was confined to clashes between the socialists and the conservatives, and with each subsequent clash the number of rioters increased and the number of injuries soared. Fear reigned across the country, gun sales spiraled, and the ammunition for numerous calibers of weapons was getting harder to find. Both sides were armed, but neither mob had opened fire on the other during the demonstrations—at least not yet.

* * *

On his return flight from the FBI's terrorist lab in Huntsville, Alabama, Detective Mike McShane looked out at the cloudy sky at 8,000 feet and thought about Senator Bainbridge's death.

He was a powerful Socialist who had been working in conjunction with the newly elected president, Luther Garcia, by trying to convince Republican senators that Marxism was the answer to the nation's problems, particularly in light of the continuing financial chaos caused by the infiltration of millions of undocumented aliens. Most of the illegals had already registered as Tri-Party adherents in the sanctuary states and cities, and to make matters worse, the Wuhan virus was again rearing its ugly head all across the country. However, Marxism was a hard sell for the Tri-Party since the conservatives held the majority in the Senate along with the backing of untold millions of American citizens who abhorred socialism.

*Senator Bainbridge and Mayor Alverez*, Mike thought, *may have been targets of opportunity for an individual who is allegedly determined to preserve our government as a constitutional republic, since it is obvious the Tri-Party seems unwavering in its attempt to turn America into a socialist nation like China, Laos, Vietnam,*

*Cuba, and increasingly Russia. All the other Russian government officials resigned after Putin wanted to change the country's constitution. All those countries are ruled by dictators who now call themselves eternal presidents to ameliorate the reviled title of dictator!*

*Maybe the sniper was now haunting New York City because it somehow determined its next target had to be the mayor of a large sanctuary city,* Mike continued to ponder, *since the chance of assassinating the president or a left-leaning governor was virtually impossible, as security for those prominent politicians had recently been bolstered in every state in light of the near murder of President Trumpmeyer, the recent turmoil between the leftist radicals, the American Eagle Militias, and the murder of Senator Bainbridge. However, slaying the mayor of a large sanctuary city might produce the same intended result of killing a president or a senator, which is to instigate a second civil war! But who would want that?*

*The mayor of New York had been an avowed Socialist, a member of a growing and well-established force ostensibly determined to change our form of government. By killing a few local criminals first, the sniper may have masked his true intent of killing more prominent politicians and dupe the FBI and the NYPD as to who his true target was.*

*If so, the sniper's actions now made the mayors of other major sanctuary and non-sanctuary cities possible targets—revenge targets in the case of the non-sanctuary city mayors. Is the sniper working alone or could the rumors of a shadow government be a real possibility? Is there a cabal that is so well trained and organized that it has escaped the detection of all our federal intelligence agencies?*

However, the matching bullets from the Bainbridge, Rico, and Alvarez assassinations seemed to prove otherwise to Mike, since it indicated the sniper was working alone. By the time the wheels of the jumbo jet touched down on the runway at LaGuardia, Detective Mike McShane dismissed the idea of a shadow government as a mere figment of someone's overactive imagination.

# CHAPTER 3

---

Detective Mike McShane knelt on the Saint Joseph's side of St. Hedwig's Roman Catholic Church with his wife Gloria and looked up at the crucifix above the altar, praying to God for a clue to the sniper's identity. Moments later as he sat listening to the sermon delivered by Father Ramon, he looked over at the nuns seated in the front two pews on the Virgin Mary's side of the nave; both seats were full.

The parish and Saint Hedwig's school was growing. Most of these new parishioners were undocumented aliens or their children. Many couldn't speak English, and so the cardinal of the Archdiocese of New York authorized the parish to hire lay teachers, who were proficient in Spanish and English, to teach the aliens America's native tongue. Mike knew some of those English as a second language teachers were also undocumented aliens.

When the Mass was over, Mike and Gloria were discussing the current announcements from the Vatican that were disclosed during Father Ramon's sermon.

"The Holy Father has condemned President Trumpmeyer for building a border wall to keep undocumented aliens from entering our country," Mike said, "and he blesses President

Garcia for reopening the floodgates on our southern border to again admit the poor and oppressed masses that are apparently fleeing the most destitute and oppressive countries of the world."

Although the McShanes are devout Catholics, the pope's attitude presented a rather perplexing problem for them. "On one side of the coin," Mike said, "the Holy Father is condemning President Trumpmeyer for building a wall to protect his country against an invasion force rife with criminals of every description, and the many others that are infected with  a plethora of diseases that had almost been eradicated in the United States. On the other side of the coin, the Holy See is living in palatial splendor in Vatican City that is surrounded by a wall eight feet thick and 40 feet high. It is also defended by an army of Swiss guards! I know it is the world's smallest city state and yet . . ."

"It just doesn't compute," Gloria chimed in, "President Trumpmeyer is protecting his country in exactly the same manner as the pope is protecting the Vatican."

At that moment, the Mother Superior approached them on the church steps to inquire about the progress of the investigation into the mayor's murder and that of the drug dealer, Pedro Rico. But just then another nun was passing by, and Sister Clarinda reached out and gently seized her arm.

"Sister Mary Theresa, this is Detective Mike McShane and his wife Gloria. As you know, he is heading the investigation into the murders of Mayor Alvarez and Pedro Rico."

"So nice to meet you both, Mr. and Mrs. McShane," Sister Theresa said as they shook hands. "We're offering up our prayers in hopes you'll catch this person soon."

"Thank you," the detective replied. "We need all the help we can get."

*She has the most alluring smile*, Mike thought.

"As you know Detective, our staff is growing," the Mother Superior said, "and Sister Theresa just transferred here from Los Angeles to help us out.

"Sister Theresa," the Mother Superior continued, "Detective McShane, Gloria, and their three children all attended Saint Hedwig's school at one time or another. They are lifetime members of the parish."

"That is so wonderful, Detective," Sister Theresa replied as she smiled at him again. "It was so nice to meet you both."

"Likewise, Sister Theresa," Mike and Gloria replied in unison. Then the nun excused herself so the Mother Superior could continue her private conversation with the lawman and his wife.

"I'm afraid I have nothing new to report, Sister Clarinda," the detective said. "Please tell your staff to be extra careful, especially those ESL teachers. We have no idea what else this psychopath may have on his mind."

As he was approaching his car, Mike's cell phone rang. It was a tech from the NYPD police lab in Queens. "Sir, I have something here I think you need to see. It may be a break in the case."

"I'll be right there, Hal," he hastily replied.

After he dropped Gloria off at home, Mike drove over to the lab even though it was a Sunday morning. He pushed his way through the glass doors marked "NYPD Lab" on Homelawn and 171$^{st}$ Street in Queens and asked the tech, 'What have you got, Mr. Schrantz?'"

"Here's our boy, Detective," he replied.

"I don't see anything," Mike said as he stared at the screen.

"There," Hal pointed to a barely visible silhouette on the frame of the video screen.

Mike leaned closer, and there in the shadows of a building on 49$^{th}$ Street he spied a ghostly figure clad in dark clothing. The eerie unsub was standing close to the wall, seemingly unconcerned by the passing foot traffic.

"I searched through hundreds of hours of films yesterday and today," Hal said, "and picked this up on a storefront camera on 49$^{th}$ Street. It was shot on the night of the Rico murder."

"Well I'll be damned," the excited detective muttered as he slapped the tech on the back, "great work!"

"Wait and watch what happens next, Detective."

Hal rolled the film again and a car stopped near the curb to drop off an apartment resident, and the tech stopped the film again. The added illumination of the car's headlights posed a slightly more distinct outline of the figure.

Mike looked closer then pointed at the image and said, "What the hell is that thing sticking up from of the back of his head?"

"It took me a while to figure that one out, Detective, but there is nothing sticking up from the back of his head. That's the muzzle of a rifle slung across his back and the end of the barrel extends slightly above his head."

"It's too big to be the tip of a rifle barrel, Hal. A weapon of that caliber would have a bore the size of a grenade launcher."

"No Sir, what you're seeing is the silencer."

"If that's true, he wouldn't be able to see the front sight."

"He's using a sniper scope and therefore doesn't need to see the front sight blade, Detective." Mike McShane was a combat veteran and he knew that a long time ago but forgot about it.

Mike looked at the tech with his thick blond hair and wire-rimmed glasses and knew he was right. He wasn't even 25 years old, and yet he was already one of the sharpest techs in the NYPD lab.

"Watch what happens next, Detective."

He rolled the film again and as the car pulled away from the curb, the woman passenger blocked the camera lens for a moment; when she strolled out of sight, Mike's jaw dropped. The shadow had disappeared.

"Where the hell did he go?"

"I don't know, Sir, and I checked every entry and exit camera in the building for the 24 hours, but he doesn't appear on any of the tapes either arriving or leaving, and then I monitored those films for the 48-hour period before the cameras recycled the films."

"Maybe he lives there," Mike responded, "get me the address."

Twenty minutes later, Detective McShane entered the alley he saw on the film and immediately noticed the gate. It was black and not visible on the film. *He must have gone through it,* he mused. But when he peered between the metal bars, he realized the alley ended at a pair of emergency exit doors bearing a sign, "Caution. Alarm Sounds When Doors Open." There were no handles on the outside of the metal doors and he didn't hear any such warning sound on the film the tech showed him, although he could hear the faint hum of traffic passing by.

"The man never exited by the alley or opened the emergency doors," he mumbled to himself.

That left only one option: he had to climb up the side of the building. He recalled the words the snitch told him, "An elusive shadow that moves silently through the alleys and up the sides of buildings and jumps from rooftop to rooftop."

The thought spurred his resolve, and a moment later Mike was standing exactly where the mysterious figure stood on the night Rico was killed. He looked up. All the windows on the first floor had security bars, and the second story windows were too high for anyone to reach them. Then he noticed something unusual. The corners of the ornate apartment building were made of square concrete pillars covered with sheets of glossy granite that extended all the way to the roof. *But no human being could possibly scale those smoothly polished surfaces,* he mused, *because there aren't any hand grips or niches anywhere.*

He took a deep, exasperated breath and walked out of the alley to the other side of the building. That alley was narrower than the one on the other side and the adjacent building had a fire escape. He looked up and noted both buildings had flat roofs and that a low parapet ran around the entire perimeter of the first building.

*It wouldn't be easy*, he pondered, *but a daredevil athlete with a good running start could clear the wall and the gap between the buildings. If he shot Rico from the rooftop, then the fire escape on the adjacent building would provide a quick and safe getaway route, but how in the hell could he get to the top of the building in the first place? Well, it's Sunday. I better get home and spend some time with Gloria.*

Then his phone rang again. It was the lab tech again.

"Detective McShane," he said, "we missed something important on the tape."

Fifteen minutes later, Mike was looking at the frame where the shadowy figure had disappeared.

"Look at the extreme upper right-hand corner of the frame, Detective; see that little dark spot?"

"Yeah."

"Well Sir, I got a couple of other lab techs to look at it too and we enhanced the image; it is the toe of a boot."

"That's impossible," Mike almost shouted, "those granite-covered pillars are as smooth as glass."

They called the FBI lab in Quantico, Virginia.

"Yes," the agent said, "we've had several cases where criminals climbed smooth stone walls or glass-enclosed buildings by using round rubber disks attached to their hands and legs. But it is risky and requires a lot of practice, especially with the ones secured to the knees.

"The disks are similar to toilet plungers. You push them against the smooth surface to make a sealed vacuum to hold your weight. The handheld ones have a release valve so you can break the vacuum with the press of a finger and move your arm to the next position. On the knee disks, you push outward to break the vacuum so you can move that leg up, and therefore the climber must always keep the knee on his other leg pressed inward to maintain the seal on that disk, and you can only move one limb at a time. Otherwise, having only two disks to support your entire weight might cause you to fall."

Mike McShane was delighted. The pieces of the puzzle were slowly being pieced together.

* * *

The Eagle heard the news from his informant in the FBI and it was not good. A Republican Party state representative had been gunned down by several masked men in a drive-by shooting as he left his home in Olympia, Washington. The car they used was later found abandoned. It had been stolen. The rep's sponsorship of HB 1109 would make the harassment of any public officials or their families a state crime, and it was scheduled to be debated on the House floor the day after his death. Consequently, the bill was never debated, not even by other Republicans in the House, who were too frightened to bring it to the floor, and therefore it was never voted on.

In another suspicious incident, a GOP Oregon state senator had mysteriously disappeared a week ago, leaving behind a wife and three children. His burned-out car—with his body inside—was discovered in a wooded area not far outside of Salem. The actual cause of his death was yet to be determined, although the use of an accelerant to ignite the interior of the vehicle was suspected. His pending legislation was identical to that of his murdered counterpart in the State of Washington, but now it too would never be brought to the Senate floor for debate. The undeclared civil war was picking up steam, but the national mass media didn't air it to make certain the American public remained in the dark.

The general American public was growing uneasy with all the other chaos in the sanctuary states that was inundating the country, and gun and ammunition sales were still at an all-time high. A US senator had been killed, and now the mayor of a large metropolitan area had been murdered in broad daylight. Both were Democrats, and their deaths were reported by every major news outlet in the country.

However, the deaths of the two Republican state legislators in Oregon and Washington were confined to local news stories. Even so, the pro-democracy elements in those two states remained staunchly loyal to the cause of liberty. It was obvious to them that the Socialists—the Tri-Party—was behind the whole fiasco, and that by not reporting the deaths of those two Republican legislators on their national news outlets, the mass media was upping the political ante.

The Eagle looked at his watch; it was five thirty a.m. *She is right on schedule,* he thought, as he followed her movements through the Scout Sniper daytime scope. When she and her companion reached the top step of the studio, he pulled the trigger.

* * *

It was his day off, and Detective Mike McShane wanted to spend the day at home with Gloria and his son Junior. His two daughters were away at college and the family had planned to call them on Skype, but his phone rang at seven a.m. It was Captain Andreas, the Central Park Precinct commander.

"Earlier this morning, the sniper killed former Secretary of State Hilary R. Minton!" he said.

"Oh my God," Mike blurted out. "Isn't she the one who was involved in that controversial deal debacle that gives Russia 20 percent of the uranium that is mined in the United States?

"Yup," the commander replied, "and her Minton foundation received millions of dollars from the Russian government for it."

"And wasn't she involved in causing the death of the American ambassador and several other Americans in Benghazi by refusing to send military aid to rescue them?"

"You're right again, Detective McShane!"

"Didn't she and the DNC also pay for the fake dossier on President Trumpmeyer a while back and was never prosecuted for it?"

"Yup, she's one and the same," the captain replied.

"What the hell was she doing in New York City?' Mike asked. "I thought she lived in Chappaqua. That's about 30 miles outside the city."

"She does," the captain answered. "But Congresswoman Rita Moreno was getting ready to appear on CBS news to announce her candidacy for a US Senate from New York. Minton was going to appear on the show to lend Moreno her endorsement. The whole thing was supposed to be an exclusive broadcast."

"How did the sniper know she would be in New York if her appearance was to be a surprise?"

"Obviously, the sniper has someone on the inside working with him," Captain Andreas answered, "and that really complicates matters. Oh, by the way, the FBI just released the shooter's profile with the aid of the tape we shared with them, courtesy of their Behavioral Analysis Unit. He's a white male between five feet eight and five feet ten inches tall, weighs about 165 pounds, and is between the ages of 25 and 40; he is most likely an ultra-right-wing conservative with a military background."

"I'm not surprised about his military background, Captain."

"Yeah, me either. Now every cabinet member and congressional socialist, progressive, and liberal is going to demand Secret Service protection until this guy is caught. You and I know that's not going to happen, Mike. However, Mayor Sandoval has already pledged that in light of the Minton slaying, the NYPD will provide a security detail for any elected Tri-Party official or political candidate when they're in the city."

Detective Mike McShane wiped his brow with his handkerchief. He knew he wouldn't be spending the day with his family after all.

# CHAPTER 4

The first socialist president of the United States, Luther Garcia, gazed out of the Oval Office at the South Lawn of the White House. In 2021, he became the first Hispanic and the first Socialist to be sworn in as POTUS by a narrow margin, since President Trumpmeyer was still recovering from the knife wound that nearly killed him. The assault occurred just days before the 2020 election and the general public did not want to elect a man that the mass media was portraying as barely clinging to life, in spite of the Republican Party's counterclaims concerning his recovery.

"It was the only way I could win the presidency," he confided to Vice President Pablo Ramirez, "and thank God the mass media outlets supported our efforts by massive displays of headlines and op-eds, claiming President Trumpmeyer was barely clinging to life and predicting his imminent end in a few hours—or at the very least, it marked the end of his political career.

"We won in spite of the fact the Mueller report had debunked the Russian collusion hoax concerning the 2016 presidential election," the socialist president said. The VP smiled broadly.

An investigation by the conservative factions of the House and Senate proved that the phony dossier was perpetrated and paid for by the then Secretary of State Hilary Minton and the Democratic National Committee. The ill-fated fake profile and the lies perpetrated by high-ranking FBI leaders in order to obtain Foreign Intelligence Surveillance Court orders to spy on candidate Trumpmeyer, and then President Trumpmeyer, eventually cost taxpayers millions of dollars. It was a waste of time and money.

The lies and deceit of the Tri-Party's impeachment proceedings in the House concerning a telephone call President Trumpmeyer made to the leader of Ukraine betrayed the desperateness of the old Democratic Party at the time. However, not one criminal involved in committing these federal crimes was ever charged—let alone prosecuted—by the Department of Justice.

* * *

POTUS knew that millions of undocumented aliens had voted in the federal election, and conservatives threatened to sue in federal court. Less than a week after his attorney general, Vincent de Leon, was confirmed, the socialist president ordered him to find a legal reason not to open an inquiry or to stall an investigation into the issue for as long as possible.

Even though the American public knew that the scam involving the voter registration of non-citizens had spread to every state in the union, Congress remained apathetic. The left-leaning mainstream news media conspired with the new Tri-Party National Committee, and they decided not to run any front page stories on the issue, so the matter was confined to mere paragraphs buried deep within the pages of the newspapers and not aired at all on the massive amount of daily electronic news releases.

* * *

"There are 340 seats in the House that I can count on for support, although our Socialist faction won only 49 of those seats," President Garcia said to the attorney general. "The difference of 291 seats is held by Progressives and Liberals, but they are solidly behind my administration. The Republicans have a mere 95 seats."

The AG merely nodded.

"Those three party elements comprise the Democratic Party that de facto no longer exists," President Garcia said, "we are now called the Tri-Party, of course, but we have to appease both the Progressives and Liberals if I am to retain their continued support.

"I'll keep my campaign promises to the Progressives and Liberals by appointing several to my cabinet and fabricate a number of staff positions for the remainder, whose friends are seeking federal employment. I'll also initiate the nomination process of Socialists and Progressives for federal judgeships, including a potential Supreme Court Justice. I have a woman in mind who is an avowed Socialist, and she will replace the ailing Associate Justice Ruth Linsberg, an avowed liberal, who is medically retiring.

"It is obvious that we the Socialists, along with the Progressives and Liberals, have to remain united under one banner," he continued, "if we are to remain in power and achieve our ultimate goal of changing the United States from a constitutional republic to a socialist nation.

"In order to do that, we need to change the Constitution," the president continued. "We'll have to convene a constitutional convention that requires a request from two thirds of the state legislatures and the approval of three quarters of those legislatures to ratify any changes. We cannot accomplish this in the Congress, since the Republicans still control the Senate, so we have got to get the majority of the state legislatures on our side. We have a good shot there, since many elected state officials in the sanctuary states are liberals, especially those in the state legislatures of the densely populated blue states."

"You are right, Mr. President," the attorney general replied.

"To help accomplish this, Pablo," he said as he turned his back on the AG and addressed the VP, "your main function throughout the next four years of this administration will be to help me convince the American public that the only way to bring down the cost of medical care, drugs, food, automobiles, fuel, and such is for the government to seize control of all the means of production, and regulate the price and distribution of all the products manufactured in this country."

"Yes, Mr. President," the VP replied.

"And Pablo," President Garcia continued, "emphasize that the rich will bear the brunt of the cost of the Medicare for

All Program. Persuade the public that socialism will raise the standard of living of the working poor and the middle class, and stress the continuing ill fate our oppressed minorities have suffered under the Trumpmeyer administration. We need more of their swing votes."

"I understand, Mr. President," the VP replied and smiled again.

The 95 House Republicans vehemently opposed the Tri-Party's proposed resolutions—one after the other—as did the Republicans in the Senate, where they held a slim majority of three. POTUS already knew he would have to rely on the state legislatures if he were to achieve his goal of eliminating the Electoral College, and changing the Constitution to elect the president by the popular vote only, and ensuring he could be reelected for five more terms. This could be accomplished only with the aid of the illegal alien voters. Any involvement of the Congress in the process would thus be a mere formality.

"The influx of millions of those undocumented aliens into the Tri-Party will ensure a conservative defeat for generations," President Garcia told the Vice President. "However, the Second Amendment still guarantees the right of Americans to keep and bear arms and it is a lingering problem; an uprising by an armed populace is possible. Only the military would be strong enough to subdue an armed mob of patriots, so in order to change my title to that of Eternal President, we will need to convince our military leaders that Socialism is in the best interests of the country and that will not be easy!"

* * *

President Garcia's campaign promise to drastically cut US military spending drew accolades from China, Russia, Iran, and a slew of smaller nations, even though he and the Tri-Party knew that decimating the military would eventually make America a third-rate power behind China and Russia. Those countries supported the Tri-Party's agenda and claimed a drawdown of America's military would be the first step in achieving a lasting world peace.

However, the impending drawdown of America's military might give China the impetus for continuing to threaten US warships patrolling the South China Sea, claiming it was a violation of its sovereignty. It had convened two maritime home courts and issued its own interpretation of maritime law concerning the waters claimed by Vietnam, Indonesia, the Philippines, and Brunei for centuries.

Their resolution differed from the international definition of maritime territorial borders of course, and the rest of the fretful world could do nothing to oppose China's provocative and aggressive declaration since President Garcia was radically reducing the size and power of America's international military presence. Therefore, the United States would no longer be the world's peacekeeper.

Russia, in turn, had announced the development of an underwater nuclear capable drone, and was building a military base in Venezuela that would put its TU-160 bombers within strike range of American soil. This would eliminate the ten-hour flight time and aerial refueling currently required to reach targets in the US mainland. Again, President Garcia refused to take a stand on the issues plaguing the Venezuelan people as he did with the escalating fiasco in South China Sea and the new Russian threats.

President Garcia's open borders policy and curtailing the number of Immigration and Customs Enforcement officers delighted Mexico and most Central American nations, particularly those with corrupt governments providing safe havens for the drug cartels that now had stockpiles of drugs since the COVID-19 threat had temporarily closed the border and their opiate smuggling had slowed to a trickle and human trafficking once again began to flourish in North America.

But President Garcia's attempts to limit gun rights guaranteed by the Second Amendment were met with the fierce resistance of the NRA, the Senate, the general American public, and the 95 minority party members in the left-leaning House. It was an uphill battle for the newly elected president and the Tri-Party advocates.

In the House and Senate, Republicans cited the warning of Thomas Jefferson, the third POTUS, whose convictions were forged at the hands of a despot, England's King George III, and his witnessing of how armed American patriots freed the fledgling nation from English bondage.

"No free man shall ever be disbarred the use of arms within his own lands or tenements" is documented in *The Jefferson Papers* and a draft of the Virginia Constitution of 1776. In fact, Jefferson's influence and insight on gun rights is so imbued in the nation's psyche that modern American scholars have merged Jefferson's caveat with another Revolutionary War patriot, Thomas Paine, whose admonition against disarming American citizens reads: "The strongest reason for the people to retain the right to keep and bear arms is, as a last resort, to protect themselves against tyranny in government."

The Second Amendment was a huge problem for the Socialists, Progressives, and Liberals since conservatives properly pointed to Thomas Jefferson's tenets on how armed patriots had freed America from the oppression of Great Britain, which incited the American Revolutionary War, and they also cited what happened to German citizens after Adolf Hitler had disarmed them when he became chancellor. Consequently, seven million human beings, including six million Jews, thousands of Catholic priests, ministers, mayors, and other uncooperative politicians and private citizens went to their deaths in the gas chambers or were executed by firearms without having a single weapon with which to fire back in self-defense.

The Second Amendment defenders also reiterated why Japanese Admiral Yamamoto, in light of his sneak attack and victory at Pearl Harbor, had nixed the idea of invading the west coast of the United States. The admiral had lived in America for years, attended Harvard University, and traveled extensively throughout the United States while he served as the Japanese Naval attaché in Washington. He knew the American public was armed and that his army would be repelled by millions of patriots who would lie hidden behind every rock and bush along the entire coastline of California.

✳ ✳ ✳

*I am the Commander in Chief of the Armed Forces,"* the Socialist POTUS thought as he sat at the Resolute desk in the Oval office, *and an unarmed American public is the crux of what I need if I am to seize and retain absolute power. But I will have to find a way to obtain the allegiance of the armed forces to ensure they remain loyal to me during the crisis that is sure to ensue once the Article V Convention nullifies the Second Amendment. I may have to pit them against the millions of armed citizens who refuse to surrender their arms despite the Posse Comitatus Act of 1878 that forbids the use of federal troops to enforce domestic policies.*

*If the convention ratifies my request to banish gun ownership, disbars the Electoral College, and at the same time allows the president to serve for six consecutive terms, then I will go down in history as America's first 24-year president! However, if the convention also ratifies the change of the federal government from a democracy to a socialist nation, then I will not have to concern myself with those other three issues, since the old Constitution will no longer be the law of the land and I will be president for life; an eternal president!*

He savored the thoughts of a one-party system, the Tri-Party, dominating the US government, and the resultant dictatorship that defines the management of all socialist governments, even though he knew no such nation in the history of the world had endured the test of time. He openly scoffed at the conservative ideology—"He who does not study history is bound to repeat its mistakes"—that illustrates the limited duration of socialist governments and the poverty and suffering that ensues.

* * *

President Garcia knew the fate of Germany during Hitler's Third Reich, and the current fate of Russians, Cubans, Chinese, Laos, and Vietnamese. Those countries were prime examples of what happens to the unarmed citizens of nations ruled by dictators. Those governments do not believe in the God-given rights of man as espoused by the American legal system, which is founded upon Judeo-Christian principles. It was the political power and the glory President Garcia and the left so fervently desired, not their love of the freest and most glorious country the world has ever known, whose divine destiny has rested for more than 244 years on that parliamentary bedrock known as the Constitution of the United States.

* * *

"The alignment of the Tri-Party, Antifa, the BLM radicals, and the Boogaloo Bois makes for strange bedfellows," Mike told Gloria at dinner one night. "On the one hand, the leftist Tri-Party allegedly wants to change our constitutional government to a socialist one ruled by a single party and an eternal president such as the one that exists in China; Antifa, the very far left-wingers, want an anarchy with no federal government and laws that are made by a conglomeration of different groups of people; and the Boogaloo Bois are far right-wingers who fear the government will confiscate all the private citizens' arms—and they maintain law enforcement needs to be abolished and that only an outright civil war can serve as a means to that end. Many of its members are white supremacists and believe the civil war will be a race war, which astounds me as to why the BLM has formed a coalition with either the Antifa or the BLM radicals.

Mike never noticed Gloria's tight-lipped grin as she listened to his story. *He's learning,* she thought!

* * *

An incident happened during Trumpmeyer's tenure in office. It was the perfect opportunity for the far left and the far right to form a weak axis, with each faction hoping the outcome would favor their own specific ideology.

A white police officer killed a black man, who was restrained in handcuffs and not resisting arrest, by deliberately kneeling on his neck, even though the victim kept repeating that he could not breathe.

The murderous incident sparked a national outrage, even though the police officers involved were charged with murder and other various crimes. All across the nation, protests continued and turned into riots that ended with burning buildings, looting, beatings, and murder. Hordes of demonstrators marched and carried signs reading and chanting "Black Lives Matter," and during those riots radical members of the BLM took control of the movement.

Some black leaders openly condemned the violence, but others did not. The Democratic Party leaders aggravated the uprising by refusing to condemn the riots and hoping to destroy the administration of President Trumpmeyer in the

November elections by sweeping Republicans from offices all across the land.

But the outbursts went far beyond demonstrations, and it soon became obvious that the leftists, Democrats, Antifa, the BLM radicals, and the Boogaloo Bois were deliberately keeping the riots going, and the chaos was funded by the millions being poured into the façade's coffers by Democrat billionaires George A. Schultz and Thomas Flyer.

An open civil war was at hand, and it was the perfect time for the three loosely organized factions of the Tri-Party to strike by keeping the insurrection going: the left-leaning Democrats wanted socialism to prevail; the extreme far left, Antifa, wanted anarchy and the destruction of capitalism; and the far right, the dangerous Boogaloo Bois, wanted law enforcement destroyed and a race war. Those three factions intended to keep the current agitation going until their goals were realized and the greatest threat to their existence—President Trumpmeyer and his administration—was deposed through violence or was destroyed at the polls. Once that happened, the Tri-Party triad could then turn on each other to accomplish each faction's individual goals.

* * *

From its perch atop St. Patrick's Cathedral, the amber-eyed Eagle scanned 5th Avenue through the Scout Sniper daytime scope. It was the route that Socialist billionaire, George A. Schultz, would take while en route to speak at the Tri-Party, Antifa, Boogaloo Bois, and the radical BLM political rally at Rockefeller Plaza.

George Schultz was born into a wealthy Jewish Hungarian family that survived the Nazi occupation of his homeland, and at the end of WWII his family immigrated to England and then the United States, where he worked at various jobs in finance and in the stock market while amassing a fortune.

He was a Socialist who had labored diligently but fruitlessly to defeat Republican presidential candidate George W. Bush in favor of Al Gore in the 2000 presidential election by donating millions of dollars to the Democratic cause, and he also was a staunch supporter of Hussein Abdul Ogama, the first black POTUS, whose familial allegiance to Islam belied his proclaimed Christian ethics.

Later, Schultz threw his wealth and support behind presidential candidate and former Secretary of State Hilary R. Minton, who supported and financed the creation of a fake dossier in an attempt to destroy the election of Ronald J. Trumpmeyer, a staunch conservative and later the duly elected Republican president. It was a disaster because the conservatives exposed the dossier and other bogus reports that were paid for by the Democratic National Committee and candidate Minton with the full support of several top-ranking officials of the FBI, most of who were fired when the scam was exposed.

The 2016 election results made billionaire Schultz hate President Trumpmeyer even more, whose popularity had crested with his motto, "Make America Great Again." Trumpmeyer's philosophy swept the country and it made him the most powerful and successful president in modern history.

The economic boom and tax reforms he had initiated created millions of jobs for all races of Americans and raised the welfare of the average citizen by utilizing the principles of capitalism.

Under President Trumpmeyer, the employment of women and minorities had risen to an all-time high, and his protection of American citizens against the unfair trade practices of other nations, and the tariffs they imposed on American goods and services, were monumental achievements. The rogue dealers of the horrific American trade imbalance included allies in the European Union, Canada, India, Mexico, South Korea, and Japan, but most specifically China.

Their blatant violations of the World Trade Organization rules were an international disgrace that no other American president had ever addressed, but President Trumpmeyer did by imposing tariffs on those nations. Those accomplishments were but a few of his triumphs and they kept his popularity at a zenith with the majority of American citizens.

Then, in an attempt to destroy the American economy in retaliation for the United States imposing tariffs on its goods and services, the Chinese Communist Party unleashed the Wuhan Virus on the world. It dulled the strong American economic stream created by President Trumpmeyer, but he reacted quickly and decisively to contain the evil, much to the chagrin of the old Democratic Party that was desperately clutching at this opportunity to destroy his administration and the American way of life.

The fake Russian dossier didn't work; the phony impeachment trial held by the then Democratic Party didn't pan out; the lies about his phone call to the President of Ukraine didn't work either; the Democratic presidential candidate of their 2020 election bid, Bo Viden, was struggling with dementia, which had to be kept hidden from public scrutiny as much as possible; the Wuhan virus didn't work; and now the old Democratic Party was clinging to and promoting a nationwide insurrection—its one last frantic hope of regaining its lost political power—and they were hoping the funds provided by George Schultz and his ilk would keep the chaos going until the 2020 election.

Then tragedy struck with the near demise of President Trumpmeyer just days before the 2020 election. The Tri-Party retook the presidency and kept the House but did not win the Senate. But it was the perfect time to intensify the fear in grassroots America and keep the turmoil in the country going until two thirds of the state legislatures agreed to convene an Article V Convention.

George A. Schultz had also contributed millions to President Garcia's election campaign and was largely responsible for the demise of the party once known as the Democratic Party. It became the Tri-Party in deference to the Socialists, Progressives, and Liberals that now dominated its ranks. Socialist upstarts Cortezy and Omary had brushed aside the once-powerful Speaker, Mandy Melosi, and ever since a struggle for control of the House was in full swing. Melosi, fearful of losing her status as the most powerful woman in the federal government, ceded her power to the Socialist by embracing their leftist ideology.

The Eagle clandestinely learned from the conservative spy in the Garcia administration that Mr. Schultz's current visit was designed to overtly sanction the Socialist's ideology, which was to continually apply force to obtain results that they did not accomplish by elections or the rulings of the left-leaning federal judges. Force was the sole option the left felt if it were to achieve its ultimate political aims via an Article V Convention. Unofficially, the plan had already been indoctrinated along Tri-Party lines by the leaders of the Democratic Party factions with the loss of the 2016 elections, which triggered the onset of open hostilities toward conservatives in the United States.

Antifa, the strong-arm enforcement wing of the Tri-Party, initiated their terrorist tactics by getting in their political opponents' faces, terrorizing conservatives and their families, engaging in beatings, traffic jams, rapes, and attempts to intimidate them at polling places during elections—and even outright murder.

Although Trumpmeyer's goals were also the alleged aims of the Socialists, Progressives, and Liberals, their methods of achieving those ends were antithetical. The Progressives wanted a mixture of socialism and capitalism, while the Socialists sought the outright demise of capitalism. George A. Schultz and Thomas Flyer kept funneling millions more into the coffers of the socialist element of the party, but the American Eagle knew socialism was the mother of progressivism and a prelude to communism.

*While both those factions seek the equality of all members of society,* the Eagle mused, *their approach is rather different than that of a democracy. Socialists desire that the government must run and control the production of all goods and services in the country, as well as the distribution of its products, for the so-called welfare of society. Capitalism, they believe, exploits the working class. This requires them to abolish capitalism through elections, by judicial decisions, or by force if necessary.*

*Progressives, on the other hand, do not condone violence,* the Eagle pondered, *but they want to gradually improve the status of the average citizen, and not just the working class, by voting Progressives into power and strictly regulating businesses. Thus, their aims are to form a mixture of progressivism and socialism by drastically controlling the wealth of a few. However, both socialism and progressivism are prologues to communism, a pathway to dictatorship, which is not the American way.*

Unfortunately, the conservatives lost the 2020 election by a very narrow margin of electoral votes to Luther Garcia, an avowed Socialist. Trumpmeyer could not continue his reelection bid because of his serious wounds. The Eagle knew from the surveys taken by political action committees that most of the American people did not understand socialism or progressivism, and yet both of those blocs had gained enough traction in all 50 states to elect a Socialist to the presidency.

*I,* the Eagle thought, *am a patriot, and like the continental soldier of old, I have taken my musket in hand to defend my country against the evils of tyranny. President Garcia is leading our country down the path to communism and destruction; no socialist country in the history of the world has ever prospered. Therefore, I must do my part and fight the enemy from the outside, just as the socialists are trying to destroy my country from within by force.*

*We are in an undeclared civil war, and although I can't get to the president like the socialists did to President Trumpmeyer, I can neutralize some of Garcia's efforts by silencing the other crucial members of the socialist, progressive, and liberal movements, just as Antifa is doing against conservatives. I, and patriots like me, can also rid society of the key drug dealers and the human traffickers at the same time, who are poisoning and enslaving our youth. They are our upcoming leaders and the patriots who must someday take my place and resurrect our democracy from the grave in which the Tri-Party is trying to bury it!*

* * *

The May sunshine heated the space beneath the canvas camouflaging the Eagle as he lay nestled behind the cross between the two towering spires of Saint Patrick's cathedral. The cover blended in well with the color of the roof, making it difficult to spot his hide from the air. It was stifling beneath the canvas, but the Eagle had borne many such challenges of extreme temperatures during his three tours as a sniper in Iraq and Afghanistan.

As the Eagle straddled the ridge of the roof with one leg on either side, he felt a twinge of pain in the old thigh wound that had earned him a Purple Heart and a Bronze Star with a Combat V. The Eagle and the enemy sniper had fired at each other at the same instant, and both had hit their targets, but the ISIS fighter was dead.

This hide was in an awkward location but provided the Eagle with the only clear shot between the buildings on Fifth Avenue. He would have to fire to his extreme left toward West 49th Street to hit his target.

It was a weekday and luckily only one member of the clergy was in the cathedral, so the Eagle easily avoided detection. He glanced down at the maintenance door on the balcony. He picked the lock several hours ago and left the door slightly ajar to be certain his escape route was easily accessible. Then he peered out from beneath the arms of the cross atop St. Patrick's Cathedral and noticed the foot traffic was increasing. The crowd was heading for Rockefeller Plaza, where the Socialist, George A. Schultz, was scheduled to speak in a few minutes.

He heard the familiar whomp whomp of a police helicopter overhead. It was patrolling the area around Rockefeller Plaza, but it didn't detect his hide and soon passed on by. There was a multitude of buildings in this area that kept the NYPD air crews busy, while on the street below their counterparts in police cruisers rode down Fifth Ave and turned onto West 49th Street to where the crowd was forming.

Although he couldn't see them, the Eagle knew that dozens of heavily-armed patrolmen and a dozen canine handlers were protecting and controlling the throng gathering in the plaza. Thousands of threats had been called in to the NYPD demanding the Tri-Party-sponsored rally not be held, and since Antifa, the Boogaloo Bois, and BLM radicals would be present in significant numbers, the liberal mayor also dispatched police explosive experts and their bomb-sniffing dogs in order to ensure the further safety of the demonstrators.

Then the Eagle spotted a police sniper on the Saks Fifth Avenue building directly across West 50th Street, and several others on the roof of the Longchamp Leather Goods and Michael Kors Design Apparel shops. His farther view was blocked by the mass of buildings so he couldn't see beyond them, but obviously the entire block of the Rockefeller Business Complex was being protected by a ring of their best counter-fire snipers, the foot patrolmen, and the sharp-shooters in the police helicopters that were constantly circling overhead. It was the NYPD at its finest!

The Eagle looked at his watch. It was 11:20. His sources told him Schultz's limousine would be passing by the cathedral at 11:30. The Eagle moved the AR-16 forward so the hand guard rested against the upright stem of the cross, and then he looked up Fifth Avenue and was startled to see the flashing red and blue lights of a line of approaching police escort vehicles. The convoy was a few minutes ahead of schedule so he had to act quickly

The first two police escort vehicles passed through the width of his Scout Sniper daytime scope and then the hood of the limo came into view. As the vehicle slowly crept toward the plaza, the head of the passenger in the back seat appeared in the scope; ti*ghten your grip; center the reticle; wait for the kick*, flashed through the Eagle's mind.

He felt the kick, and the rear window shattered into a glass spider web when the bullet struck, but the limo kept on moving, still signaling a right turn on to West 49th Street, still heading toward the plaza.

The Eagle was shocked and thought, *I missed!*

The car came to a jarring halt when the driver heard the sudden blare of the sirens from the trailing police cruisers, and his eyes fearfully shifted to the rearview mirror. The slumped figure and shattered rear window were clearly visible through the glass privacy window separating the front and rear compartments. The driver's trembling hands quickly began fumbling with his seat belt. Then he frantically flattened himself onto the passenger's seat and slid onto the floor and stuck his upper body beneath the dashboard as far as he could, with his quaking hands covering the back of his head and his body shaking uncontrollably. It was a terribly frightening experience for a 20-year-old millennial Socialist!

The Eagle quickly gathered up the canvas sheet and the rifle and skidded to the edge of the roof before jumping down to the balcony and then dashing towards the maintenance door in the church's left spire. He hurried inside and closed the door just as a police helicopter appeared and hovered over the church for a few moments, while its airborne sniper scoped out the roof before the chopper moved on to check out the next building.

The Eagle removed his outer clothing and opened the valise he stowed on a cross beam when he entered the spire, then buckled the specially-designed belt around his waist. Then he hastily buckled the rifle to the belt, slipped into his everyday work clothes, and then moved between the labyrinths of timbers before quickly descending the staircase leading to a hallway. It ran the length of the church and he briskly walked until he reached the door leading to the sacristy. He opened it slightly and breathed a sigh of relief when he discovered the lone clergyman was not there.

He then entered the chancel and his right knee touched the floor as he genuflected at the altar before opening the gate leading to the nave. Then he quickly knelt down in one of the front pews and clasped his hands in pseudo prayer. A few moments later, a frantic horde bounded through the main entrance, fleeing the horror of the sniper, and right behind them came two armed policemen.

"The sniper just killed George Schultz," a woman shouted as she looked down at the praying Eagle. "Please pray for him."

"Oh no," the Eagle replied, "may God have mercy on his soul," and then he made the sign of the cross and bowed his head.

"Amen," the woman softly answered.

"Has anyone seen any suspicious person run through here?" one of the officers asked.

"No," several people in the crowd answered.

One of the officers stopped and glanced at the praying Eagle for a moment, but then he kept on walking. The officers searched the chancel and the sacristy, the choir loft and both spires, and when the search proved fruitless, they left by a side door. After the crowd settled down in different pews and began praying for the Socialist or softly chatted about the horrific incident some of them had just witnessed, the Eagle reached down and seized the valise hidden beneath the pew. Then he quietly and quickly exited the nave by the same side door the police used and anxiously glanced at the frenzied scene.

The street was abuzz with foot patrolmen, police cruisers with flashing lights and blaring sirens, and the tempo of several helicopters whirling above the plaza. Several paramedics had emerged from a fire engine and were examining the victim, but it was too late. The man was dead and the police immediately took control of the crime scene. The Eagle quickly turned away and walked down the street to the subway entrance. Once again, he had to get back to work before anyone discovered he was missing.

* * *

Agent Sara Glitz, head of the FBI office in New York City, and Detective Mike McShane, the NYPD's lead investigator in the sniper killings, peered in at the body slumped over in the back seat of the limousine.

"He was a billionaire patron of the Tri-Party in the United States," Sara said.

"I know, and we'll be depending on the FBI for a lot of support. Our resources are spread pretty thin right now with all these killings going on."

"We have a full complement of manpower available," she replied, "which is rather surprising considering . . ."

"Considering what?" he asked.

"The spate of murders that is happening all across the country," she softly said. "There were almost a thousand last month."

"But murders fall within a state's power and not the federal government's jurisdiction, Sara."

"I know that," she said, "but if you promise to keep your mouth shut, I'll tell you what the problem really is all about."

Mike was taken aback; *the problem?* he thought.

But as he gazed into her dark brown eyes, he realized she was going to trust him with some information she wouldn't ordinarily disclose to anyone outside the bureau. She was a pretty and petite agent, but she had a reputation for being as tough as nails when she had to be.

"Alright," he finally answered, "I'll keep my mouth shut."

"Good, Mike. Most of the murder victims are locally-known grassroot conservatives," she whispered, "and we are certain they are being murdered by members of a single gang operating across state lines, so those crimes do fall within our jurisdiction. We suspect Antifa, who are anarchists, and they are an organization of prime interest since they believe in force if they cannot win an election or judicial rulings that are not in their favor."

Mike's jaw dropped. He was a historian of sorts and knew the story of Antifa and that they were relatively unknown and not politically active in the United States as far as he knew.

"The killings started right after President Trumpmeyer was nearly stabbed to death," Sara said, "by that White House staffer on the Domestic Policy Council, Office of Social Innovation and Civic Participation, which is a branch of the White House staff that was created by the Ogama administration. The would-be assassin is a hold-over from his administration, and he is being hailed as a hero by the left.

"However, the attorney general, Vincent de Leon, issued a confidential memo that says the FBI will not initiate any investigations of those lesser-known murders under any circumstances, since we can't prove who is behind them," she said. "The AG says murder falls under a state's jurisdiction, and that this memo is classified and is not for public release."

*Classified*, he thought? *She just broke a cardinal rule of the Bureau, but why is she confiding in me?*

"Why the hell don't we see or hear about this on the news or from NYPD Intel?" Mike asked.

"It's like President Trumpmeyer said many times before," she replied, "Do not trust the fake news media or the governors and mayors of the blue states. The mainstream media will never report any news without the Tri-Party's stamp of approval. They began throwing their support behind the Socialists, Progressives, and Liberals years ago—you know that, Detective."

Mike had a hard time believing what she was saying about the multitude of slayings, even though everyone knew the mainstream news media outlets had always reinforced leftists' viewpoints, and they made no bones about hating President Trumpmeyer.

*But she is FBI rank and file*, he thought, *and those agents are amongst the most loyal and patriotic Americans.* He was too skeptical and too shocked to say anything else.

"Why don't you stop by my house this evening around seven?" she softly said. "I have a lot more things I would like to discuss with you." Then she slipped him a piece of paper with her home phone number on it.

Once again, Mike was flabbergasted. *What does she want to talk about something in private that can't be discussed openly with the NYPD?* he mused.

* * *

Detective McShane knocked on Agent Glitz's condo door and was soon sitting on the sofa clutching a cup of coffee.

"The man who attempted to murder President Trumpmeyer, Jose Feliz, claimed he was angry," Agent Glitz said, "because anyone entering the country at that time was being forced to use the ports of entry as dictated by federal law, and he claimed his family members were vetted and rejected because of his political affiliations with the Democratic Party. He alleges they were stranded on the southern side of the border far from their homes in Central America, but all that proved to be a lie.

"He was born in Nicaragua, raised as a Catholic, and has always been an avowed Socialist. Later, he converted to Islam and eventually joined a fundamentalist group. As you know, he was convicted of the attempted murder of President Trumpmeyer and sentenced to life in prison without the possibility of parole.

"However, the American Civil Liberties Union immediately came to his defense, stating that the attempted murder wasn't his fault, and although they acknowledged that President Trumpmeyer had always acted within the parameters of his constitutional powers, his rhetoric on illegal immigration incited many Socialists, Progressives, and Liberals to violence.

"Consequently, after Jose Feliz was found guilty, Antifa went on a rampage. There were confrontations, beatings, riots, and shootings in every state of the union, which overwhelmed local police forces, and now we suspect those same people are behind this murder spree of conservatives. Yet there is still no federal investigation, and the mainstream media has remained silent on the issue."

Mike stared at Sara. There was nothing in the mainstream news media about any alleged nationwide assassinations by the radical arm of the Tri-Party, but they were publicly ascribing blame to the conservatives for the recent spate of sniper killings. Only the attempted murder of the president occupied their headlines for weeks, so what she said seemed unreal, and yet he knew what she told him could get her fired or even prosecuted.

She sensed his skeptical gaze and said, "I would like to introduce you to someone, but first I must ask you to place your Smith & Wesson 640 on the table." Her request startled Mike.

"Why?"

"I don't want you to go off half-cocked."

"It sounds as though you want me to trust you with my life?"

"I do, Mike, just as the citizens in New York put their lives in your hands every day! But this isn't just about New York anymore. It's about the future of our country, and that's far more important than your life or mine."

He trusted her, and yet the anxiety he felt as his hand gripped the handle of the pistol in his shoulder holster was almost overwhelming; apparently someone else was in the condo! For more than 20 years, he was armed no matter where he went in New York; even when he went to bed at night, his old trusty .38 caliber S&W was never beyond his reach even when the kids were little. As he laid the pistol on the table, Agent Glitz slowly reached across the table and then grasped it.

"I feel rather vulnerable," he said.

"You are," a strange voice echoed from somewhere behind him.

Detective McShane jumped off the sofa and spun around, his hand clutching at the empty holster inside his jacket. "Who the hell are you?"

He stood face to face with a figure clad in black and wearing a hooded mask over his face. His voice now sounded somewhat familiar, but the mask disguised his true identity. Mike recalled the shadowy figure on the tape the lab tech showed him.

"You're the sniper!" the detective shouted, and suddenly Mike McShane felt very naked.

"No Detective, I am not. Let's just say I have served the American people in various military and political positions for the last 30 years, and at the present time I am serving in another rather sensitive capacity."

"If you aren't the sniper, then you must be one of his informants," the detective reasoned. "That is how the killer knew the exact time and route Mr. Schultz was taking while en route to the rally at Rockefeller Center Plaza, and when and where Hilary Minton would appear before you helped murder her."

"That is somewhat correct, Detective," the dark clad figure replied.

"You are guilty of duplicity and complicity in their murders, Sir!" Mike shouted.

"I understand your wrath, Detective McShane, because you don't know the whole truth," the mysterious stranger replied.

"I don't know the whole truth about what?" the detective retorted.

"Raise your right arm and swear you will never divulge what I am about to tell you!"

"I will never swear allegiance to whatever a murderer has to say to me!" Mike retorted.

"When you graduated from the Police Academy, you stood with your fellow officers and swore to protect and defend the Constitution of the United States, enforce its laws, and to protect the people of the City of New York, remember? This is about the security of our country."

The figure had moved across the room and now he stood just a few feet away, his eyes seeming to be burning into the soul of Mike McShane through the eyelets in the hooded mask. Keeping an oath meant a lot to Mike, and for a brief moment he felt a slight tremor of emotion.

"Okay, whoever you are," Mike answered. "I will swear not to divulge our conversation—but that is all."

"Fair enough, Detective." The man reached inside his black jacket and produced a small pocket-sized bible, and Mike McShane placed his left hand on it and raised the right, and repeated, "I do solemnly swear never to reveal the information that is about to be divulged to me, so help me God."

* * *

The three of them sat at Sara Glitz's kitchen table and the mysterious stranger gazed across at Detective McShane as he spoke. "We have known for a good number of years that a shadow government exists within the confines of the White House, its staff, and Congress, but thus far the Supreme Court remains untainted, and the confirmation of Justices Gorsuch and Kavanaugh were major victories for us."

"Who is us?" the detective asked. The figure hesitated for a long moment as he gazed at the NYPD detective. It was a defining moment for both men.

"Remember the oath you took, Detective McShane.'

"I will remember," Mike retorted.

The mysterious figure hesitated for another long moment; he knew he was putting a lot of faith in the man he always trusted, and yet the lives and futures of a long list of patriots would be in his hands in a moment.

"We are the Sons and Daughters of Liberty," the man slowly said, "and we are constitutionalists who want our form of government to live forever. The Tri-Party had set a plan in motion to destroy our democracy, even when they were the old Democratic Party. Our SDL principles are similar to those of the NYPD; enforce the laws according to the Constitution, preserve peace, reduce fear, and provide a safe environment for all Americans."

"So you are saying for certain the Tri-Party will forcibly tear our federal government apart if they can?" the detective asked.

"Absolutely," the masked stranger replied. "They have seized the presidency and legally permeated the House. Their aim is to make the United States a socialist nation like China, Cuba, Laos, and Vietnam, where the government owns and controls all means of production and the distribution of its products and services.

"Of course, socialism and progressivism are preludes to communism, but the Tri-Party can't accomplish that goal until they first disarm the American public by a constitutional convention—an Article V Convention—to nullify or modify the Second Amendment, annul the Electoral College, and allow the president to be reelected for six consecutive terms. It requires two-thirds votes of both houses of Congress or the consent of two-thirds of the state legislatures to convene a constitutional convention, and then ratify any subsequent changes by three fourths of Congress or three fourths of the state legislatures.

"The Socialists and Progressives don't have the political power to do this yet, so they must resort to covert activities until they do so, but even then they know millions of Americans will never surrender their guns. Right now, the president and attorney general are designing a clandestine computer program that snoops into the database of all 50 states to see which citizens have registered their guns and how many."

"How do you know that?" Mike asked.

"We have our sources," the hooded stranger replied.

"If an Article V Convention convenes and the Tri-Party succeeds in ratifying its agenda, the Constitution will outlaw gun ownership by all American citizens, and their Tri-Party henchmen will go from house to house to confiscate their weapons, just like Hitler did to the German people. Once that happens, only the police, criminals, and the military will be armed, and then it will be open season on the citizens who refused to surrender their guns.

"According to their plan," the masked stranger continued, "the military must remain loyal to and be under the control of the president, and he is scheming to retain their loyalty by introducing a budget that will grant them a hefty raise and more benefits even as he cuts the defense budget. To do that, the president must take money away from new Weapons System Development to give the rank and file more money. He is trying to buy their loyalty.

"That is why we need the help of people like you to preserve our constitutional form of government, but all our activities must necessarily remain covert to protect our members and our cause."

"So you are asking me to condone the killing of Senator Bainbridge and George Schultz and the others?"

"That is what our enemy is doing," the masked stranger continued. "Our only hope was to beat them to the punch, and by utilizing a sniper we are trying to force an FBI investigation into the murders of conservatives at the grassroots level as well as inquiries into our own political killings. Antifa and others haven't resorted to killing any prominent conservative politicians yet, except for the attempted murder of the president. They are killing lesser-known conservative legislators and conservative citizens at the grassroots level and disguise those murders by utilizing rival gang tactics like drive-by shootings, which rarely make the national news casts.

"Thus, the fate of those victims has been reported by the fake local news media as being collateral damage of street gang violence. That way the press won't air any news that will initiate any national attention to the killings. But of course, that's a cover-up; this has been happening for months now in Chicago, New York, Atlanta, Philadelphia, Dallas, Boston, Minneapolis, San Francisco, Baltimore, and Los Angeles, and it is spreading across the rest of the nation's blue states.

"And listen to this, Detective," the stranger continued, "the Tri-Party claims Jose Feliz acted on his own and now they've thrown him under the bus because President Garcia tells his staff that it's too early to commute his sentence yet. He may spend years in prison, but we are certain he didn't work alone. However, we can't prove it just yet."

Mike didn't say anything and yet what the man said made some sense to him.

"Antifa," the man continued, "and MS-13 gang members have formed a loose alliance with the proviso that if Antifa's bedlam is exposed, they will literally utilize MS-13 gang members to continue to intimidate conservatives and their families in the sanctuary states and cities to discourage them from running for any state or national office or for reelection at any level of government."

Mike now looked at the stranger in the hooded garb with disbelief.

"How come not a single word has been spoken or written about this in the mainstream news media?" Mike skeptically asked.

"The mainstream media is remaining silent on those issues to prevent the public from knowing and demanding any further federal investigation into any of these matters," the stranger said. "The Tri-Party now has political clout and if they gain the absolute loyalty and control of the military, they will install President Luther Garcia as an eternal president—a virtual dictator. Then the socialists will be in power indefinitely, and the mass imprisonment or killings of prominent conservatives will ensue, which is what also happened when the socialists took over in China, Cuba, Laos, and Vietnam.

"Like most Americans, you did not realize until Fox News and One America News dug into the facts that exposed the complicity of a number of government agencies. Members of those agencies are part of a shadow government in the nation's capital and are otherwise known as the swamp. They illegally spied on candidate and then President Trumpmeyer and his entire campaign via the Foreign Intelligence Surveillance

Act based on the dirty dossier paid for by Secretary of State Hilary Minton and the Democratic National Committee. The crime here was that the FBI leadership didn't tell the FISA judges the dossier was paid for by the opposition party, which is in bed with the shadow government, or that the writer of the dossier had debunked it from the start. If they had done so, the FISA warrants would never have been authorized.

"That shadow government has existed for decades in the halls of Washington, DC. It is also composed of professional bureaucrats that are not elected and can't be fired but were invested long before the advent of the Ogama administration, which these bureaucrats favored. Trumpmeyer is not a professional politician. He is already a billionaire and can't be bought by the swampers, even those in his own party—or by anyone else, in fact!

"That clandestine shadow organization is composed mostly of a number of long-term elected officials and the eternally employed and unelected bureaucrats who deem themselves as the only true professionals capable of running the country. They abhor the more recently elected officials because they consider them to be amateur politicians.

"However, President Ogama, his VP Bo Viden, Attorney General Eric Folder, and former Secretary of State and presidential candidate Hilary Minton  hold a political ideology mimicking that of the shadow government, which despises President Trumpmeyer and his America First philosophy. They are the swampers the nation keeps talking about and they are making hundreds of millions of dollars by using their influence to make corrupt deals with foreign nations for the benefit of themselves and / or their families by promising them American aid—taxpayer's money.

"That's why they hate Trumpmeyer—he's draining the swamp and can't be bought, and he never backs down. That's why they tried to kill him! He is a threat to the shadowy political infrastructure they have built. Trumpmeyer didn't owe anyone in Washington any political favors either, and therefore he is an outsider. He was a president of the people, the voters, who the swampers look upon as idiots, and they contrived to destroy him even though he was the duly elected President of the United States!

"However, the public—those so-called idiots—foiled their attempted coup by electing Trumpmeyer president via the Electoral College. The Democrats then concocted that dossier and convened a Special Counsel to discredit candidate and then President Trumpmeyer. After two years of investigation, the Special Counsel couldn't find any evidence that Trumpmeyer conspired with Russia to rig the 2016 election as avowed by the Democrats.

"An exposé disclosed the phony dossier and yet no action has ever been taken by the Department of Justice to prosecute the perpetrators who concocted the lies and illegally spied on the Trumpmeyer campaign with the aid of a former British Intelligent agent named Christopher Steele.

"Then of course there was the Ukraine phone call that alleged President Trumpmeyer had conspired with the Ukrainian President to have former Democratic vice president

Bo Viden, a 2020 presidential candidate, and his son, Bunter, investigated.

"Bunter was already under investigation by the Ukrainian attorney general for alleged corruption involving the gas company Burisma, one of the largest energy companies in Ukraine. By using his political position as leverage, Bo Viden, the then Vice President of the United States, publicly threatened to withhold billions of dollars of American aid to Ukraine if the investigation of Burisma and his son continued. Consequently, the Attorney General of Ukraine was fired by the corrupt president of Ukraine in order to receive the billions of dollars in American aid.

"Bo Viden became a strong Democratic Party contender, and the Democrats then accused President Trumpmeyer of initiating an investigation into his candidacy during that telephone conversation with the president of Ukraine, concerning that corruption in his country. The Democratic Party then initiated that phony impeachment inquiry against President Trumpmeyer with the intent of removing him from office. It didn't work of course. The House impeached him but didn't have the power to remove him from office. That would take a trial and conviction by the Senate, which the Republicans control.

"The impeachment investigation was done in secret and with testimonials from a list of anonymous whistleblowers but did not include any Republican congressmen. Since the testimony was kept secret, President Trumpmeyer and his supporters were not given the opportunity to rebut the testaments of the clandestine whistleblowers, a clear violation of congressional procedure.

"However, the information taken from a string of witnesses eventually proved the Tri-Party's evidence to be mere hearsay, idle talk, which can be defined as evidence from a source other than that actually heard or witnessed by the person providing the so-called evidence.

"As you are aware, Detective," the hooded stranger said, "that proved to be another scam that did not bode well for the Democrats. The president's chief antagonist, Senator Sniff of California and Chairman of the House Intel Committee, got caught with his pants down with his pack of unsubstantiated claims and lies, and he emerged from the witch hunt with a red face and a red butt from the proverbial ass kicking he received from the president and the general public.

"When those measures also failed, the old Democratic Party then deemed the Electoral College as being outdated, since Trumpmeyer had won the 2016 election over presidential candidate Hilary Minton by garnering the majority of electoral votes, and they fear this might happen to President Garcia in the next election.

"The Tri-Party leaders knew that most of the millions of undocumented aliens pouring across the border were bound to register with their organization, and so those politicos stymied conservative efforts to control the flow of illegal immigrants into the US by refusing to grant funds for a border wall.

"The Tri-Party hoped their numbers that were swelling their roles in the sanctuary states would be enough to force two thirds of the state's legislatures to convene an Article V Convention and pass legislation to abort the Electoral College, thereby forcing any future presidential candidate to be elected by a popular vote if their efforts to change the country into a socialist nation nosedives. That would mean a few densely populated blue states would control the election of a president for decades to come, which would negate the votes of all the other states.

"However, since our forefathers realized that a few heavily populated states would exert dictatorial control over all the other less populated ones, they wisely assimilated the Electoral College into the Constitution. Thus, the Demoncrats, as the old Democratic Party had been dubbed by the conservative American public, were determined to keep the southern border open to swell the populations of the major sanctuary states.

"They also wanted to nullify the Second Amendment to disarm the American public unless their attempt to change the US into a socialist nation is successful. If that measure was ratified, all the other stipulations in the Constitution they abhor would be moot points, since the original Constitution would no longer be the law of the land.

"Thus, the president would then be elected by the popular vote only, ensuring that the ballots of a few heavily populated blue states would forever dominate the politics of the entire nation! The nation's citizens would also be unarmed with no guarantee of being protected from government tyranny, which will force all Americans to dwell in a country ruled by an eternal president—a dictator.

"If the Demoncrats can maintain the flow of illegals by keeping the southern border open until they got the desired number of voters needed to install a one-party political system, America would be ruled by a single party like those in power in China, Cuba, Laos, and Vietnam. Although the head of the Russian Federation claims the title of president, he is de facto a dictator, since he surreptitiously eliminates political opponents unmercifully, even those who flee to a foreign nation.

"If the United States became a Socialist country ruled by an eternal president,, unelected bureaucrats, and corrupt elected officials, the government would hold dictatorial powers  over the nation. It would be a tyrannical government. However, even though there are an untold number of corrupt officials in our American democracy today, they are currently held in check from seizing absolute political control by the current US Constitution, which defines the power between the executive, legislative, and judicial branches of our government."

* * *

The whole idea was mind boggling for Detective Mike McShane, and he struggled with the notions of the Sons and Daughters of Liberty throughout the night—yet what the stranger told him coincided with what he did hear on Fox News and One America News, and the next morning he headed for the NYPD Queens lab and pulled Hal Schrantz aside. It was a ruse, but he had to know the truth.

"You're the computer guru, Hal, and I have an idea I want to run by you."

"What idea, Detective?"

"Don't you think it would behoove us to take the serial number on every gun manufactured in the United States, the type of weapon, and the names of the registered owners, and put them into a central data bank? Then we could link our database with the networks of all the other states and trace the ownership of a gun from the day it was manufactured until law enforcement had custody of the weapon—or at least we would know who the original owner was so we could trace its current whereabouts."

Hal Schrantz cringed and put his finger to his lips as he looked both ways to make certain no one overheard the detective's remark. "Where the hell did you hear about that, Detective?"

"I didn't hear anything," Mike softly whispered back, "it was just an idea that I had."

"Well, Detective," Hal answered softly, "get it the hell out of your head and don't mention it to anyone—and anyone includes your family! If the wrong person ever heard us discussing any such thing, we would both lose our jobs and face prosecution—and that comes straight from Governor Como's office!

"I have been developing a program to coordinate the transfer of all our known data about registered gun owners in the State of New York to the FBI lab in Huntsville, Alabama, but it's a hush-hush job. It is supposedly part of the federal government's anti-terrorist program and will eventually be enforced nationwide.

"Even the Deputy Commissioner of Internal Affairs doesn't know about it, so if there is a leak the mayor will deny he authorized any such activity, and anyone involved could be branded as a rogue technician, and I'd be up to my ass in shit. So don't ever mention your idea to anyone ever again—not even another lab tech!"

Detective Mike McShane was horrified! What the tech said dove-tailed with what the mysterious stranger told him last night about how Hitler had everyone in Germany register their guns allegedly for their own safety and then had his henchmen confiscate all their weapons. What the Socialists were preparing to do in America was exactly how Nazi Germany disarmed its private citizens!

*However,* Mike thought, *upon my graduation from the Academy, I took an oath to protect and defend the Constitution of the United States and the citizens of the City of New York. If—and it is a big if—it turns out that the Sons and Daughters of Liberty are correct about the Tri-Party's true intent to forcibly turn our democracy into a socialist nation, then I may have to  choose between my country and my city. If I choose to remain loyal to my country, can I, an NYPD detective, condone the killings of some of the citizens I have sworn to protect?*

The doubts taunting his mind lingered, but he finally said to himself as he headed back toward the Central Park Precinct, "Nah. The SDL is too radical in its thinking." But then he remembered the warning President Thomas Jefferson and Thomas Paine, the patriot, said about an armed populace:

"the main purpose of an armed citizenry is, as a last resort, to protect against government tyranny."

For some reason, the thought upset Mike McShane and he again thought about the new government gun ownership registration database being developed in radical states like New York. *That is exactly what Hitler and the National Socialist German Workers' Party—the Nazis—did to its citizens,* he thought, *and it is now the blueprint of what the Socialists, Progressives, and Liberals in the Tri-Party are trying to do in America!*

"He who does not study history is bound to repeat its mistakes," Mike McShane, a self-proclaimed amateur historian, mumbled to himself as he entered the parking garage.

*Our country has been a democracy for more than 244 years,* he reassured himself, *and nothing can change that, not even a socialist president.*

*A Second American Civil War,* he mused, *would be insane,* and he nearly shivered at the thought of the horrible consequences he knew would follow—and for the first time in his life, he said to no one in particular, "The majority of our native born citizens would never stand for a socialist government takeover!"

Then he suddenly halted in mid-stride and was flabbergasted when he realized he was mollifying his own lingering doubts. "American citizens would never stand for it, but resisting a socialist government takeover would be a civil war," he continued to say aloud, "because like the Revolutionary War Patriots of yesteryear, today's American citizens are also armed, and the warning of our forefathers about the tyranny of government is as pertinent today as it was in colonial times.

"The proof is in the pudding—dictators like the kings and queens that ruled nations during the Middle Ages; Germany under Hitler just 80 years ago; and China, Russia, Cuba, and Vietnam today, and perhaps Venezuela in the future, are all ruled by Socialists, and those countries are all in turmoil!"

Several people coming into and going out of the parking garage briefly glanced at the well-dressed middle-aged man standing there and talking to himself. He wasn't even wearing a COVID-19 mask.

*But he doesn't seem to be a threat,* they pondered. Native New Yorkers were used to the dozens of crazies like him wandering about the streets of the city every day.

# CHAPTER 5

The months flew on by, and it was a bright sunny day on July 4th. The 843 acres of New York's Central Park were humming with activity in spite of the intensifying turmoil that was roiling the country.

Joggers and bikers shared the 58 miles of pedestrian trails, and the 30 tennis courts were alive with bouncing balls and agile players. All 26 ball fields were packed with opposing teams. The shouts of encouragement and cheers by their supporters echoed across the meadows to where hundreds of other Manhattanites were rambling about or embracing. Many laid on a multitude of different colored blankets, napping and idling away the holiday. Others were alone and walking about or lying on the grass, enjoying the balmy summer breeze and listening as the wind was rustling the leaves of the 20,000 trees dotting the landscape.

However, the holiday celebrants were not alone. Mounted uniforms from the Central Park Precinct were patrolling the paths and byways, and motorcycle cops rode up and down the six miles of roads. A SWAT team, stationed at precinct headquarters, was ready to react at a moment's notice in case of trouble, while their compatriots in several helicopters traversed the skies above the park and the rest of the city, ready to report any unusual activities. They had to be on alert.

These were troubling times in America, where the forces of communism—the Tri-Party—were struggling for absolute political power in the sanctuary cities and states like New York. It was in those cities and states that Antifa, the Tri-Party's enforcement arm, continually clashed with a new organization known as the American Eagle Militias. This new group was supposedly an underground organization that had suddenly sprung up along with another one of the NYPD's counterterrorism units that covertly came to be known as the SDL: the Sons and Daughters of Liberty.

The SWAT team was well aware that the Socialist National Committee chairman, Lance Freeman and his girlfriend, Beth Malking, were spending the Fourth of July holiday in NYC, and might be harassed by the SDL or even perhaps that other faction known as the American Eagle Militia, although its activities thus far had been confined to providing security at conservative political rallies. But since the NYPD was here in force, everyone felt safe. It was a typical American Fourth of July holiday.

The Loeb Boathouse had lines of people waiting to lunch at the famous eatery, and many of its 100 row boats were already on The Lake. Lance Freemen and Beth Malking were patiently awaiting their turn to rent one. They didn't want to attract any attention, since this was their clandestine getaway weekend from the hustle and bustle of Washington, DC, but the mystery and apprehension of the sniper had not yet been resolved, and so secrecy was their refuge.

The NYPD pleaded with the couple not to venture out on The Lake, as they would make tempting targets for an expert marksman such as the sniper, but Lance Freeman felt secure behind the confidentiality of their visit and their disguises, and insisted on going anyway. The park was one of the major attractions in the city they wanted to see, and Beth had never been on a boat ride. Besides, it was an opportunity for Lance to impress his female companion with his daring and courage. He hid his identity beneath a wide-brimmed hat and wrap-around sunglasses, while Beth, a devout Presbyterian, disguised herself as a Muslim and shrouded her cheeks and forehead with a hijab.

Fifteen minutes later, Lance rowed out past the crowded Bethesda Terrace, and then beneath the cast iron Bow Bridge that was jam-packed with hordes of holiday revelers heading in both directions. Not far behind the couple was a covert security detail, consisting of an armed male and female police officer who were pretending to be a casual loving couple enjoying the federal holiday.

From his hide on the 23rd floor of a luxury hotel beyond Central Park West, the amber-eyed Eagle scanned The Lake through the rifle scope. The intelligence unit of the national SDL got a tip from its high-ranking informant within the Garcia administration that the couple planned to spend the weekend in New York, and described how they would be disguised.

Beth Malking was black and the NSC chairman was white, and the Eagle was flabbergasted when he discovered several other couples fitting the same exact description and profile were also on The Lake.

*It's a defensive tactic,* he thought, *drummed up by the NYPD counter-intelligence team, and the chairman of the National Socialist Committee probably made a concession to the NYPD's demand to make their visit more secure. I am willing to bet the other identical couples in the boats are cops in disguise, who are putting their lives on the line for a scumbag Socialist. If I kill the wrong person or if I don't fire because I cannot identify my quarry, it will be a socialist victory!*

The Eagle watched for more than an hour until two boats caught its attention. Boat Two lagged behind Boat One, but with every stroke of the oars the second one seemed to shadow the movements of the first, even though at times their bows were pointed in different directions.

*Boat Number Two might be a security detail,* the Eagle mused.

Yet he still couldn't ascertain the true identity of his prey. It had to be the right hit because he might never get another shot at the National Socialist Committee chairman if he missed or killed the wrong person. In all his tours of being a Special Forces sniper in Iraq and Afghanistan, he had never mistaken the uniqueness of his intended kill or snuffed out the life of an innocent civilian, and on a few occasions he never pulled the trigger because he was uncertain as to the true identity of his intended victim. However, both boats moved farther north on The Lake and were soon out of the M16 rifle's 600-meter maximum effective range, but they were still visible within the scope.

The essence of a sniper is patience, and the Eagle waited for more than two hours until both boats turned about and headed back down The Lake toward the boathouse. As they were approaching the Eagle's line of vison from his perch on the inside windowsill of his hotel room, the woman turned her head toward the shore and he caught a brief frontal glimpse of her face. He quickly glanced at the photos lying next to the rifle, a picture of Beth Malking with a hand-drawn hijab depicting what she would look like in her disguise and what the SNC chairman looked like in a wide-brimmed hat and sunglasses; a voice whispered within his psyche, *it's them!*

The Eagle set the scope two clicks to the left to counteract the northern breeze and poked the muzzle through the tiny hole in the bottom right-hand corner of the window that he had so cautiously removed with the glass cutter. Only the tip of the muzzle fit through it, and he peered through the scope and the part of the glass window that remained intact, and recalled the words in his psyche that had guided his hits so many times before; *tighten your grip, watch the reticle, wait for the kick.*

The blessed peace of the revered holiday was suddenly shattered by a series of frenzied screams echoing across The Lake in Central Park. Everyone stopped and gazed westward, wondering what was causing the stranded woman to scream so frantically! The crowd crossing over the Bow Bridge came to a halt, customers at the Loeb Boathouse gazed toward The Lake's edge, and sightseers at the Bethesda Terrace shaded their eyes from the late afternoon sun.

Moments later, they saw a police helicopter hovering above a boat that was rocking from side to side with the woman's every frantic move and horrifying scream. She held her head between her hands as she moved about the small craft, but there was no place to hide and she couldn't swim.

The curious crowd watched as another boat approached and quickly pulled her aboard. It was obvious the couple in the second boat were using their bodies to shield her. While the female officer laid the frantic woman down to make her a more difficult target and covered her prostrate form with her own body, the male officer jumped into the boat they were shadowing and examined the victim. He saw the horrible head wound and knew Lance Freeman was dead.

"This is Central Park Tactical Unit One," he blurted over his radio.

"Central Park Tactical Unit One, K," the station dispatcher responded.

"10-13; victim shot on The Lake; shooter unknown; possible location a high rise on the West Side."

"10-4, Central Park Tactical Unit One; medical unit and SWAT team are on the way."

"10-4," the officer in the boat responded.

A few minutes later, a police launch with several paramedics and a SWAT team on board arrived, and the victim was officially pronounced dead.

The on-scene officer said they were directly across from 74th Street when the victim was hit—probably from a high-rise—and 20 minutes later, a SWAT team member inserted the electronic key into the slot on the door of Room #5341 of the luxury hotel.

When the several SWAT team members suddenly burst through the door, a woman screamed and covered her partially naked body with a black dress as the officers pointed their rifles at her before scanning the rest of the room with their weapons. She was soaking wet and had a towel wrapped around her head. It was obvious she had just stepped out of the shower. But the officers continued their search and cleared the other two rooms of the suite.

"Sorry ma'am," the senior officer said, "but we're searching for the New York sniper. He just killed another victim."

She looked too startled to reply.

"Suite #5341 all clear," the officer said into the radio mic as he closed the door.

As soon as the door closed, the Eagle removed the towel from around his head and stuffed the wet blond wig into the valise hidden beneath the bed. Then he dried himself off and pulled his underwear back on before buckling on the special belt and fastened the M16 to it. Afterward, he put on his everyday clothes and peered both ways down the hallway. While the SWAT team officers searched another suite, the Eagle took the elevator to the ground floor, checked out of the hotel, and quickly walked toward the nearest subway entrance.

* * *

The SWAT team searched every room of several hotels, but the sniper was nowhere to be found. It was extremely frustrating, and Mike McShane ran his fingers through his hair. *The SWAT team didn't apprehend a single suspect or turn up the slightest clue,* he mused. He was exhausted and that evening he sat down to watch the 10:00 report on FOX news.

"... in light of the murder of Socialist Party National chairman, Lance Freeman," the commentator said, "citizens and some members of the NYPD are again demanding the resignation of Police Commissioner Robert Hereford, and the removal of Detective Michael McShane as the lead investigator in the sniper killings. Mayor Phil Sandoval declined to comment, and there is a growing national concern of murder-for-hire schemes being perpetrated by both political parties... In other breaking news, President Luther Garcia announced his intention to scale back military spending by another $400 billion dollars for the upcoming fiscal year, although he will raise the pay and benefits of active duty, Reserve and the National Guard troops.... He also announced the drawdown of another 100 Border Patrol Agents... Socialist Speaker of the House, Mandy Melosi, said her party will introduce legislation that gives all the states the right to officially declare themselves Sanctuary States, and allow their governor to declare undocumented aliens as citizens of those states.... The statute would also allow the POTUS to run for office for an unprecedented six terms ..."

The news that the mayor might force the PC to retire, and that he could be replaced as the lead investigator in the sniper killings, was very upsetting to Mike McShane.

*But the real shocker,* he thought as he abruptly stood up, *is that the rest of the broadcast was exactly what the Sons and Daughters of Liberty had alluded to. I wonder who is feeding them the information. The Socialists, Progressives, and Liberals wanted to give the states unprecedented powers, including the power of the Border States to make the illegal aliens citizens of those states, refuse to allow their National Guard units to be used to help the Feds secure their borders, and permit the president to run for office for six consecutive terms, which comes very near to declaring him an Eternal President, something that would require an Article V Convention. That legislation, if passed, would virtually assure the existence of a one-party system in the United States: the Tri-Party!*

"Then those extraordinary powers granted to the state's legislatures versus the inherent powers of the federal government would be unprecedented," he said aloud, "and the rest of that legislation, combined with the backing of the active duty, National Guard, and reserve units all backing our socialist president would allow the Tri-Party to be able to convene a Constitutional Convention, an Article V Convention, at the request of two thirds of the state legislatures.

"If ratified, those laws would empower the governors and legislatures of the left-leaning states to enforce the Tri-Party's intent to convert the country into a single-party system and eventually nullify the Second Amendment. It would also make President Garcia an eternal president with the authority to rescind the Electoral College as well, even though it and the Second Amendment are inherent parts of the Constitution of the United States!

"The Tri-Party couldn't depend on the Congress to pass such legislation," he continued, "because the Republicans still control the Senate. But three fourths of the state legislatures could ratify the changes, and make it possible to disarm the citizenry, just as the socialist governments of Nazi Germany, the Putin Regime, China, Laos, Cuba, and Vietnam have already done in their countries."

Mike knew that President Thomas Jefferson, and the patriot Thomas Paine, had warned Americans that the primary purpose of the Second Amendment is to protect American citizens from the tyranny of government. Those two patriots had lived under the oppression of King George III of England and knew only too well what a despot would do to the God-given rights of mankind.

Mike also remembered what happened in Venezuela and the United Socialist Party of Hugo Chavez. *He ruled the socialist country from 1999-2013 as an Eternal President, but he died in 2013 and left the population of Venezuela on the brink of starvation.* Thomas Paine's warning raged through Mike's psyche again: *the purpose of an armed citizenry is to guard against the tyranny of government!*

* * *

Detective Mike McShane couldn't sleep and sat on the edge of the bed with one arm resting across his stomach and the other massaging his forehead to ease the migraine lingering above his eyebrows.

"What's wrong, honey?" Gloria asked him as she got out of bed, walked around to his side, and sat down to console him.

"It's just work—lots of issues."

"Like what?"

"Well you know the country is so divided; the hatred is so unreal, and people in the big cities are afraid to walk the streets because of all the murders, and now the mayor is defunding the NYPD like the mayors of so many other cities are doing. And now this sniper thing I'm investigating is putting a lot of pressure on me and the department. The mayor is being pressured to retire the police commissioner, and I might be replaced as the lead investigator in the sniper case."

"Don't worry, honey, the mayor may force the PC to retire, but he will never replace you as his chief investigator in the sniper case."

"What makes you so sure?"

"You are very zealous in your pursuit of the sniper, and you treat the illegals with respect. You're very loyal to the mayor and the governor."

"Of course I am loyal to the mayor and the governor," Mike replied, "but so is the police commissioner. I have slaved for this city for more than 20 years and the commissioner for more than 30. We took oaths upon our graduation from the Police Academy to obey the lawful orders of our leaders and to protect all New Yorkers, remember?"

"But aren't you forgetting something, Mike?"

"Like what?"

"You also pledged your allegiance to your country! The day is coming when you may have to choose between your city and your country."

"I know. Lately I've been getting those feelings and it tears me apart. Now I know how millions of Americans must have felt when the American Civil War broke out. They had to choose between their state and country. Luckily, we are not in an open civil war."

Gloria looked at him apprehensively but didn't say anything.

"However, that civil war was fought along geographical lines," Mike said. "It was north versus south. But with the confrontations that are happening now, there is no line of demarcation; it's guerilla warfare so you don't know who the enemy might be, just as it happened during the Vietnam War. It could be your father, or your mother or brother. Then to top it off, an FBI agent tries to get me to join this secret organization that believes this president is preparing to effectively change us from a democratic form of government to a socialist government by the power of the states rather than by a vote of Congress, and she claims they'll do it by force if necessary."

"What organization?"

"They call themselves the Sons and Daughters of Liberty," he blurted out, "and the FBI Agent is named Sara Glitz. She invited me to a meeting at her house to meet a guy whose voice sounds familiar, but he was wearing a disguise. They are obviously a subversive organization and that's illegal. They should be arrested, but I swore on the Bible I wouldn't tell anyone about the organization, and that includes you too, honey, so don't say anything. I'm still debating whether to call the FBI Director, Alex Coombs, and have Agent Glitz fired or arrested."

"But you took an oath, Mike."

"I know, Gloria," he said. He sounded a little irritated at her reminder of the oath he took. "Well, they should be arrested anyway!"

"Well, then you may as well arrest me and your son too, Mike."

"What are you talking about, Gloria?"

"I knew I would have to tell you this sooner or later, Mike," she said as she stood up and turned to face him, "and now is just as good a time as any I guess. Junior and I are both members of the Sons and Daughters of Liberty and I trust you not to betray us!"

"What?" he shouted as he came bounding off the bed with his face reddening in anguish. "Are you crazy. The FBI will put you and Junior in prison if they find out. For God's sake, Gloria, he's only a senior in high school."

"Yes, he is only a senior in high school and I'm damned proud of him!" she answered. "He is more of a man than you know, Mike!"

He walked to the end of the room and grabbed the dresser for a moment when his knees weakened, and then he turned and looked at her in disbelief.

"I admit what is happening in the House and Melosi's proposal doesn't look good, but it will never pass in the Senate."

"No, it won't Mike, but two thirds of the state legislatures might call an Article V Convention and endorse the House's proposal."

"But you and the SDL are acting like we're already in an open second civil war, Gloria! There isn't any mass fighting in the streets; there aren't any bombs going off; there's no food or gas rationing; there is no draft; in fact, there isn't any open hostile shooting activities between two armies going on anywhere in this country; not even Antifa and the American Eagles have fired a shot at each other."

"No, we are not in an open civil war, Mike," she answered, "but we are preparing for it just as the Socialists are doing."

"Oh yes, Gloria, I know we've had some raucous demonstrations involving Antifa and some high-profile shootings, but not open civil war!"

"You're wrong, Mike—open your eyes. We virtually are in a civil war. It started when the Democrats wouldn't accept the 2016 voting results of our duly elected president so they tried to kill him! They also didn't accept our Supreme Court Justices that the Senate confirmed.

"It started when their constituents were encouraged by their leaders to confront Conservatives in public and bully them, gang up on individuals, spit at people, and beat them up. Antifa went to their homes, terrorized their families, destroyed their private property, blocked traffic, and all the while the liberal mayors and governors in the sanctuary states forbade their police forces to intervene.

"Your loyalty to the city is blinding you, Mike. It's a city that no longer cares about its legal citizens—the people you put your life on the line for every day. Well, I and your son are willing to put our lives on the line too, and not just for the city, but our entire nation and our way of life."

She was as angry as he was, but she wasn't finished yet.

"There is a civil war going on, Detective, but you're blinded by a loyalty to a city government that no longer gives a damn about you or your family. It's about the unconstrained political power of the Tri-Party!"

Mike was now too stunned by her anger to say anything.

"Did you ever hear of Jack Minzey or David Greenfield?" she asked.

"No."

"I thought not. Listen to what they say about a Second American Civil War."

Mike's mouth dropped open when she went over to her dresser drawer and pulled out several pieces of paper hidden beneath several rows of her neatly folded panties.

"Jack Minzey died on April 8, 2018. He was head of the Department of Education at Eastern Michigan University and wrote numerous books on education and the role of government in that regard. Jack was a conservative politician and I will read his magnificent quote that actually paraphrases a speech given by David Greenfield, an Israeli. He is now an American citizen and lives in Los Angeles.

He gave this enthralling dialogue at a Tea Party rally in January 2018.

### How Do Civil Wars Happen?

Two or more sides disagree on who runs the country. And they can't settle the question through elections because they don't even agree that elections are how you decide who's in charge. That's the basic issue here. Who decides who runs the country? When you hate each other but accept the election results, you have a country.

When you stop accepting election results, you have a countdown to a civil war.

Mike was so flabbergasted at what Gloria was reading that he interrupted her: "Where the hell did you get that?"

"I can't tell you," she answered.

"The hell you can't!" he angrily replied. "What you're doing is against the law and I'm a cop."

"So what are you going to do, Mr. Policeman? Are you going to arrest your own family?"

Mike was so shocked by her retort that he blushed and turned away. He couldn't believe what he just said to the woman he loved more than anyone else on the face of God's green Earth! *Me—have my own family arrested!* he pondered.

The thought was so numbing that he had trouble believing how he felt for even a fleeting moment. His unwavering dedication to the NYPD and the City of New York had caused his unconscious mind to conjure up a thought as horrifying as selling his own family down the river! For a brief moment, a vision of Riker's Island, that notorious jail, disrupted his already clouded thinking, and he heard Gloria still talking in the background, but he couldn't comprehend what she was saying.

"You're not even listening to what I'm reading, Mike," she angrily snapped at him.

Mike appallingly turned about to face her. His face burned still with shame and he never felt so disheartened in all his life. He wanted to hold her to assure her that he would never do that to her or anyone else in the family, but she kept right on talking and he had to listen.

"You've become so closed-minded and blinded by your dedication to the NYPD and the city that you're denying the reality of what is happening to our country. You need to open up your mind and your eyes and see what the Tri-Party is doing to our country, which is more important than any one city or one state."

He was so hurt and surprised by her retort that he didn't know what else to say, but the pain in her voice made him realize that what she was reading was very important to her; then she continued reading.

> The Mueller investigation was about removing President Trumpmeyer from office and overturning the results of an election. We all

know that. But it's not the first time they've done this. The first time a Republican president was elected this century, they said he didn't really win. The Supreme Court gave him the election.

He listened for a moment and then he regained his composure, and at that moment his detective's instincts came to the forefront of his mind and he couldn't keep his mouth shut any longer.

"What are you advocating, Gloria?" he asked.

"Can't you see it, Mike?" she answered. "We are locked in a civil war as I said, but your vision doesn't extend beyond the boundaries of the five boroughs."

"There is no civil war and no open fighting anywhere in the country, Gloria! I know that and so do you!"

"No, Mike, but it's coming. Socialists, Progressives, and Liberals are insidiously buying up arms and ammunition all across the country with the aid of the Tri-Party and its donors. They want our country to become a socialist government: free college, free medical care for all, a one-party nation—a communist nation! Socialism doesn't work, Mike. It never has and it never will! But armed American patriots defeated the most powerful nation on Earth during the American Revolution, namely England, and now we must again defend our country against the tyranny of our own government just as Thomas Jefferson and Thomas Paine warned us, and so we must never allow the Socialists to nullify our Second Amendment."

"We?"

"Yes! We," Gloria said.

"You and those people you call 'we' are perpetrating insurrection—that is, sedition and perhaps treason. If law enforcement finds out, the Feds will bring charges against you, Junior, and the other conspirators and imprison all of you."

"So be it, Mike," she shouted. "So be it! The Tri-Party is an evil that is destroying our country and our way of life, Mr. Detective, and the SDL's motto says it all: 'The only thing necessary for evil to triumph is for good men and women to stand by and do nothing.'"

At that moment, Junior walked into the room.

"Dad, what are you and mom arguing about?" he asked.

"Didn't you know you committed a crime when you joined a subversive group like the Sons and Daughters of Liberty?" Mike shouted at Junior. "Do you want to go to prison, Junior?" Mike asked.

"I'd rather go to prison than live under communism," Junior replied.

"Don't be stupid," Mike shot back. "You don't have a clue what prison is like. I do. I go there every so often to interrogate prisoners."

"You fought for our country in Vietnam, Dad, remember? That was also a civil war." Junior replied. "But this is a civil war in our country now, just like the one you fought in Vietnam. But now it's my turn to fight."

"A war," Mike shouted. "Let me tell you about war, Sonny Boy! When I was 18 years old, I was carrying a rifle for this country in that hellhole called Vietnam. I watched men, women, and children get blown to bits or bleed to death, and I held the best friend I ever had in my arms while he was dying, and there wasn't a damned thing I could do about it! I saw kids with a hand cut off by the Viet Cong because they accepted a chocolate bar from an American soldier, and children crying over a grave where Charlie buried their parents alive."

When he finished his stinging rebuke, he asked his son, "Now do you still think you are in a civil war?"

"Yes, Dad," Junior replied, "times have changed. This is not Vietnam, Dad. This war is on our home turf now! It is a different kind of civil war; it's a guerilla war! It is a battle for the heart and soul of our country, and I will not be a summertime soldier or a sunshine patriot."

"I can tell by your rhetoric that you've been indoctrinated by someone in that subversive group called the Sons and Daughters of Liberty, Junior," Mike sarcastically replied. But the high school senior didn't flinch.

"Dad," he answered, "I learned what it means to be a patriot from you. This is a war against socialism and it is tearing our country apart! You fought against the Communists in Vietnam and now it seems as though you are inviting them to take over our government and our country."

Junior's remark really hurt, and for an instant Mike recalled the risks he and his fellow Marines took every day in those swampy jungles and putrid rice patties in Vietnam. He stared blankly at his son for a moment as he recalled the expression on his dying friend's visage and the ultimate sacrifice he and others made, and he angrily slapped his son across the face.

The kid touched his cheek where the blow landed, but when Mike looked into Junior's blue eyes, he knew his son wasn't a boy anymore. *Gloria was right,* he thought, *while I was busy protecting the city for ten or twelve hours a day, my son grew into a man under my very nose and I never noticed.*

Mike realized the horror of what he had done, and he turned to Gloria with an imploring look. He had never struck anyone in the family, and she stood there with a mortified expression of disbelief in her eyes and her hands covering her mouth.

Mike started to mouth the words, "I'm sorry," but it was too late. When he reached out and touched his son's shoulder, Junior merely walked away and closed the door to his room, and Mike could tell by the look on Gloria's face that something in their relationship might have changed forever. Then for the first time ever, she smacked him across the face, then she pushed past him sobbing and entered Junior's room. It was the first time and he swore it would be the last time he would ever strike anyone in his family again.

* * *

Mike sat on the edge of the bed and looked at the clock; it was three a.m., and for the first time in more than 20 years of marriage, he knew he would be sleeping alone. He sat with his head bowed and his hand rubbing his forehead to ease the torment. *This fake civil war is tearing our family and our country apart,* he thought. *The Sons and Daughters of Liberty are probably in the crosshairs of the NYPD and the FBI, and Gloria and Junior have no idea of the tremendous resources and power those two organizations have at their fingertips.*

* * *

The next day was Sunday and the bleary-eyed detective was still horrified at his family's predicament. Gloria did not sleep with him and she and their son had not spoken a word to him. The following morning, he was shocked again when he reported into his precinct and found this memo on his desk:

### TO ALL MEMBERS OF THE CITY OF NEW YORK POLICE DEPARTMENT

The NYPD Counter-Terrorism Unit and the Federal Bureau of Investigation have identified a terrorist group known as The Sons and Daughters of Liberty that is operating within the confines of the City of New York and many other cities across the United States. Any member of the NYPD having any information concerning this little-known subversive group is encouraged to notify the FBI or your nearest precinct of the NYPD as soon as possible.

*Robert Hereford*
*Police Commissioner of the City of New York*

Mike knew the mayor had prompted the PC to issue that memo, but there was no mention of Antifa, the violent enforcement arm of the Tri-Party, and when he got off duty that day, he walked into the kitchen clasping a copy of the memo he wanted to show to Gloria and Junior in one hand, and a bouquet of flowers and a half-pound of the black licorice Junior so favored in the other. But the house was empty.

When he looked into their bedroom closet, he discovered some of her clothes were gone, and when he entered Junior's room, he could tell some of his clothes were missing too; it was devastating! He knew they feared his unwavering devotion to the NYPD might cause him to turn them in to the authorities—"but I would never do that," he sorrowfully whispered as he teared up.

His marriage was in real trouble. The bottom had dropped out of his world, and as he sat on the bed in Junior's abandoned room several hours later, the combat veteran, who was awarded a Bronze Star with a Combat V for his wartime service and now held the gold shield of a First Grade Detective in the NYPD, never felt so alone in all his life. He was just as frightened as he was when he was an 18-year-old Marine, standing in a muddy foxhole in the Phu Bai perimeter in Vietnam during Operation Checkers, where the 1st Marine Division was replacing the 3rd Marine Division that was moving close to the Ben Hai River, a natural demarcation line between North and South Vietnam.

His family had joined the SDL and would now be considered fugitives by the FBI, but what horrified him the most was that they knew and understood his loyalty and dedication to the NYPD, and they were afraid he might turn them over to the authorities. He realized that both he and his family were now victims of this undeclared Second American Civil War!

He returned to the master bedroom and picked up a copy of David Greenfield's speech that Jack Minzey had so ably paraphrased. Mike knew Gloria had purposely left it on her dresser so he could finish reading it until things had calmed down, and then perhaps she and Junior would feel safe enough to come home. Their marriage might never be the same, Mike knew, but he began to finish reading the treatise anyway, continuing from where Gloria had left off.

> There's a pattern here. What do sure odds of
> the Democrats rejecting the next Republican
> president really mean? It means they don't accept
> the results of any election that they don't win. It
> means they don't believe that transfers of power
> in this country are determined by elections.
> That's a civil war.

"It's true," he mumbled, "the old Democratic Party never accepted the results of the 2016 election, and they desperately tried to block President Trumpmeyer's nomination of a SCOTUS associate justice with allegations of sexual misconduct that proved to be false." He put the treatise down. Mike McShane was afraid to read any further. The detective feared he was beginning to understand what his wife and son tried to tell him. He teared up and whispered into the confines of the empty room, "I should have let Gloria finish reading the treatise and listened to her side of the issue. I owed her that much." Then, with trembling hands, he picked up the papers again and mused, *I'll have to be man enough to finish reading it myself.*

There's no shooting; at least not unless you count the attempt to kill a bunch of Republicans at a charity baseball game practice. But the Democrats have rejected our system of government. This isn't dissent. It's not disagreement. You can hate the other party. You can think they're the worst thing that ever happened to the country. But then you work harder to win the next election. When you consistently reject the results of elections that you don't win, what you want is a dictatorship; your very own dictatorship.

The combat veteran and NYPD detective couldn't go on; his family was right, and it was rather frightening just thinking about it. He dropped the pages back on to the bed before donning his hat and coat and heading out the door.

* * *

Mike was so distraught that he ended up at Saint Hedwig's rectory, and asked Father Jesus Ramon to hear his confession and to console him. The priest put a stole around his neck and sat in a chair facing forward, while Mike knelt at his side with his head bowed; "Bless me father for I have sinned …" and when he finished, he reiterated his dilemma.

"Father, my wife and son are members of a group the federal government proclaimed are subversive, and they fled our home believing I would betray them," he said, "but I would never do that, and yet I am torn between my loyalty to my family, my city, and my country. I don't know what to do."

"Do you acknowledge that the Tri-Party is moving our country toward a dictatorship?" the priest asked. Mike was surprised by the priest's blunt question. He was even more surprised by his own answer.

"Yeah, Father, I think it may be true."

"Well, I fled from a socialist country."

Mike's jaw dropped. He never knew that about Father Ramon nor did any of Saint Hedwig's parishioners.

"I begged God to let me live," the priest continued, "while I sought asylum in the United States, and I kept my promise to Him and became a priest. In my socialist country, we lived with false imprisonments, outright murders, and the subjugation of the entire population of Nicaragua. If in your heart and soul you believe in liberty, freedom, the God-given rights of man, and the equality of all men, then you must change your order of precedence."

"What do you mean, Father?"

The priest turned his head toward Mike and said, "You said you were torn between your family, your city, and your country. What sustained me through my ordeal, Mike, was my belief in God; that is and always will be my first priority. Then there was my family, but I have none now. They were all executed by the Sandinistas; next came my country, Nicaragua. Now it is happening here, but I am a priest and cannot fight in an army like Gloria and Junior can, and although you don't agree with them on the issue entirely, your family must be your number one priority as long as God lets you live on his green Earth. The only way I can fight now is through prayer and my vote, but as a veteran you know that sometimes the answer to your prayers can only be realized through the use of force.

"Remember your experience in Vietnam? New York, Los Angeles, Chicago, and many other cities are sanctuary cities that are supporting that socialist party, an organization that is pushing the US government towards communism—a dictatorship. Therefore, Mike, if New York City is your next priority, you will be serving more than eight million people. But if you put your country ahead of the city, you will be defending hundreds of millions of souls from the evils of tyranny. Your priorities need to be God, family, country, and then the city, Mike. God bless you and may He help you to make the right decision!"

Father Ramon's words sent Mike's mind reeling back in time to when he was a Marine and standing up to his ankles in a mud-encrusted foxhole in Vietnam on the Phu Bai perimeter. The pressure from the enemy was constant, but the Marines discovered how refreshing a few minutes of sleep could be while standing and leaning against the muddy side of their fighting holes. To sustain morale, they sang the Marine's Hymn, told the most ridiculous jokes, laughed at their own pathetic mud-covered uniforms and that of other Marines, or shouted a code of the Corps to infuriate the hidden enemy: "God, family, country, and Corps."

The priest's words echoed that credo, and although he was now a civilian and still loved the Corps, his order of precedence had to change; from now on, he mused, *My order of precedence will be God, family, country, and city.*

"I think I've got it, Father," Mike said as he stood up so the priest wouldn't see his misty eyes, and Father Ramon said, "Say five Hail Marys and one Our Father for your penance. It may help you to sustain that preference and keep you, your family, and our country safe. God bless you." Then he made the sign of the cross and forgave Mike his sins.

As soon as Mike McShane got home him, he picked up the phone and dialed FBI Agent Sara Glitz's home number.

# CHAPTER 6

---

"What made you change your mind so quickly, Detective McShane?" Agent Glitz asked as she stood there with her hands behind her back. She was suspicious and concerned that such a loyal cop might be inserting himself into the ranks of the SDL as a mole, a spy.

"I have been so concerned about protecting and defending the people of the City of New York for the last 20 years," he replied, "that I forgot about my country. It took a priest to remind me of my precedence of loyalty, and the love and courage of my wife and young son to remind me that, 'The only thing necessary for evil to triumph is for good men and women to stand by and do nothing.'"

"I am glad you reconsidered our offer," a now familiar voice said.

This time Mike turned around slowly and didn't reach for his .38, and Agent Glitz reinserted her service revolver back into the holster at the small of her back. She didn't need to protect the life of her masked compatriot.

"We know how much an oath means to you," the mysterious stranger in the black hooded disguise said, "and now you must make another oath."

Mike placed his hand on the Bible and raised the right one while waiting for the shadowy figure to administer the oath.

> I, Michael McShane, do solemnly swear to protect and defend the Constitution of the United States as written by our forefathers, and pledge my life, my fortune, and my sacred honor to my country and to protect and defend its democratic form of government from the evils of socialism, progressivism, and liberalism, by any means necessary. I pledge to preserve the God-given rights of freedom and liberty for all mankind now and forever, so help me God.

As soon as he finished repeating the oath, Mike McShane felt so very strange. For the first time in more than 20 years, the city wasn't his only sworn priority. Something much bigger loomed before him. It was all about his country again, and for a moment his mind was back in Vietnam, and once again he was standing in that muddy foxhole, cursing and shouting at the enemy snipers hidden in the distant tree line: *God, family, country, Corps.*

"You know if you break the oath and betray us that we will have to kill you," the cloaked figure said.

"I know," Mike answered.

Then the oath-giver reached up and slowly removed his hood; Mike held his breath and his jaw dropped. It was Lieutenant General Marshal Webb, US Air Force (retired) and a member of Mike's American Legion Post. Everyone knew the general was a former commander of Air Force Special Tactics—the Air Commandos.

"You are now a member of the New York City Special Ops cell, Detective McShane," the general said. "Your team leader is Sara Glitz. I will now introduce you to your fellow operatives, most of whom you know well. The room filled with the other members who filed in from the back bedroom: the police commissioner of the City of New York, Robert Hereford; NYPD lab tech, Hal Schrantz; NYPD Patrolman Kenneth Borenstein; Dr. Rita Simpson, NYPD Chief Medical Examiner; and Father Jesus Ramon, pastor of Saint Hedwig's parish."

Mike was stunned. "Father Ramon, you told me a priest can't fight!"

"I can't," the priest replied, "but there are many other things I can do like influencing my flock, writing memos, carrying messages, anonymously writing newspaper articles, and performing many other administrative duties."

Mike merely nodded when the priest finished speaking. He knew and trusted them all, and each of them in turn shook his hand and welcomed him into the SDL.

"There are two members of the cell who couldn't be here, Mike," the general said. "You will be replacing one of them and we hope you can recruit another trusted friend who shares our values."

"Who were the other two members?" Mike asked suspiciously. He knew who they were, but they were in hiding.

"This is going to be your first test of courage and loyalty to our anti-socialist group, Mike," the general continued. We think we may have a mole in one of our cells because last night the FBI raided one of our safe houses in Yonkers and arrested your wife, Gloria, and your son, Junior, among others."

There was a long moment of stunning silence when Mike couldn't speak, and he tremulously blurted out, "I tried to warn them ..." But he noticed the cell members were watching him closely. They knew his heart was breaking. This was his baptism of fire as a member of the Sons and Daughters of Liberty, and they were testing his grace under extreme pressure. Mike felt as though his life were ending, and he took a deep breath, wiped his eyes, then waited for a few moments until he regained his composure and his detective's instincts kicked in.

"Why did the FBI arrest Gloria and Junior and not the entire cell?" Mike asked.

"We don't know," General Webb answered. "But he or she must have been someone Gloria or Junior knew well and trusted." Mike couldn't think of anyone he might suspect at the moment.

"Where are they being held?" he then asked.

"Rikers Island," the general answered, "in solitary confinement."

"That's a city facility," Mike answered, "not a federal prison!"

"We know, Mike," the general answered.

"Rikers is a jail for short-term sentences or those awaiting trial for state crimes," Mike said. "What are the charges against them?"

"Sedition," the police commissioner said. "They're being charged under US Title 18, Part 1, and Chapter 115 Paragraph 2384."

"Who gives you this information? Mike asked.

"Only a very few members of the SDL know his identity," the general answered, "and it must remain so."

"Title 18 is a federal statute," Mike replied, "so why Rikers?"

"Remember, Mike," the PC said, "the Tri-Party is really the Democratic Party in disguise, and when they're in power anything is legal."

Mike suddenly recalled a passage from Jack Minzey's paraphrasing of David Greenfield's speech. It was an important part of what he now believed, but he had memorized it when his family went into hiding, and as he looked at his newfound brothers and sisters, he slowly repeated it:

> According to the Democrats, the only legitimate exercise of power in this country is its own. Whenever Republicans exercise power, it's inherently illegitimate. In 2016, the Democrats didn't win the Senate. They lost the White House. So what did they do? They began trying to run the country through federal judges and bureaucrats.

"But how can a person be legally arrested on federal charges, but be incarcerated in a state prison?" Mike asked.

"Legally, you know that a state can hold a prisoner for a limited amount of time until the Feds take custody," General

Webb said, "but that's not what's happening at the moment. The Tri-Party will hold them at any facility for as long as they please."

"Wait a moment," Mike replied, and he began repeating another part of the David Greenfield speech as paraphrased by Jack Minzey, "I think I know why."

> Every time that a federal judge issues an order saying that the President of the United States can't scratch his own back without his say so, that's the civil war. Our system of government is based on the Constitution, but that's not the system that runs this country.
>
> The Democrat's system is that any part of government that it runs gets total and unlimited power over the country. If the Democrats are in the White House, then the president can do anything. And I mean anything. He can have his own amnesty for illegal aliens. He can fine you for not having health insurance. His power is unlimited.

There was a long moment as the patriots digested Mike's words. Then Police Commissioner Hereford said, "Gloria and Junior will probably be moved to a federal institution until the government is ready to bring them to trial."

"It's a part of their scheme to move our democracy toward communism," the PC continued. "The Tri-Party doesn't want to attract any attention to their pattern. Someone arrested by the Feds usually makes the national news, but hundreds of state prisoners are confined to Rikers and other state prisons every month for whatever reason, which is not breaking news, right?"

Mike didn't answer.

"Then," the PC continued, "they can quietly transfer them to anywhere else they please. The Socialists are playing footsie with as many state governments as they can. They need their cooperation to get two thirds of the legislatures to convene an Article V Convention and are doing so by bribing them. They're granting the states unprecedented powers, such as: letting them determine their own voting laws, setting immigration policies for their states, letting them declare themselves sanctuaries for illegal aliens, and enacting treaties with other countries. According to the Constitution, those powers belong to the federal government."

Mike recalled another part of the discourse on "How Do Civil Wars Happen" that Gloria tried to read to him, and he said:

> Whether it's federal, state, executive, legislative or the judiciary, the left moves power around to run the country. If it controls an institution, then that institution is suddenly the supreme power in the land. This is what I call a moving dictatorship.
> But when Republicans get into the White House, suddenly the president can't do anything. He isn't even allowed to undo the illegal alien amnesty that Qgama illegally invented. A Democrat in the White House has 'discretion' to completely decide every

aspect of immigration policy. A Republican doesn't even have the discretion to reverse him. That's how the game is played. That's how our country is run.

Mike now fervently believed in the SDL's goals and the oath he had taken only moments earlier. The cell members talked until the wee hours of the morning, and later that day Mike McShane headed for Rikers Island to visit his wife and son.

* * *

As he approached the prison, Mike read the dreaded sign as he had so many times before that has infused terror into thousands of the newly accused and even the most hardened criminals, and now for the first time he, too, felt the fear:

City of New York
Corrections Department
Rikers Island
Home of New York's Boldest

The guard on Rikers confiscated his SIG Sauer P226 pistol and put it in the gun safe, and then directed Mike McShane to proceed to the main visitor's area.

Gloria looked rankled just as he knew she would be. She thought he had betrayed her and their son as the Feds had hoped she would in order to wring information from her about the SDL, but Mike knew she wouldn't tell them a damned thing under any circumstances.

"How could you do this to your own family?" were the first words out of Gloria's mouth.

"I didn't," he replied. "I had no idea where you and Junior were!"

"Someone did!"

"It wasn't me, Gloria. I love you and Junior."

His profession of love eased her mind and softened her expression; she knew Mike never lied. "I love you too," she almost whispered as they both teared up.

They had to be very careful about what they said, since every word of their conversation was probably being monitored and taped. In what seemed like only minutes, their hour-long visit ended, and they said their emotional goodbyes when the guard standing near her in the glass enclosure shouted, "Time's up, Mrs. McShane."

Mike stood up, but as he prepared to leave, he said, "Oh by the way, the dog misses you too." Then he winked at her with his left eye.

Gloria's jaw dropped, and as they gazed at one another for a moment she smiled for the first time since her arrest; they didn't have a dog. It was one of the cell's codes: saying something that the other SDL member knew was not true and then winking with your left eye was the last thing you did to confirm your link to the Sons and Daughters of Liberty!

* * *

When Mike visited with Junior an hour later, the kid was scared and shaken. He was a 17-year-old high school senior who had been thrust into the adult world of evil, intrigue, and sometimes death.

"The other prisoners keep yakking about what they're were going to do to my butt," he said and sobbed.

*It's a terrible ordeal for an innocent 17-year-old kid,* Mike mused, *but it's a dirty part of the American prison system. I thank God he's being held in solitary confinement so as not to be able to influence the other prisoners.*

"The FBI kept questioning me for hours and I cried at times, but that's all I did," Junior said. "I became so tired that I kept falling asleep and they banged their fists on the table to jar me awake."

The hour soon ended, but as Mike turned to leave, he compassionately said, "Grandma and Grandpa Fisher send their love." Mike noted Junior's startled expression and the detective grinned.

Fisher was Gloria's maiden name, but Junior's maternal grandparents had died when he was in the third grade. Then his father saw Junior's look of astonishment when he winked at him before the guard hustled the prisoner back to his lonely cell.

As he sat on the edge of his bunk contemplating his precarious predicament, a memory from what seemed like the distant past merged into his conscious stream of thought, and Junior recalled what he learned in one of General Webb's training sessions then bounded to his feet.

*How did dad know the code?* He thought for a moment and then mused: *General Webb would die before he ever disclosed the codes to anyone unless they were a trusted member of the SDL.*

Junior was now certain his dad hadn't betrayed him and his mom because at the time his dad wasn't a member of the SDL, and therefore he couldn't possibly have known the location of the safe house, but someone in the SDL did. The entire family was playing on the same team now, and he felt a blessed relief and a resurgence of the courage he hadn't known since the FBI arrested him.

Dropping to his knees and looking upward, he clasped his hands in prayer and silently swore to God, *I would rather die than let the cell down, just as dad risked his life in Vietnam to defend this nation and as he does every day to protect the people of New York City.*

FBI Agent Alan B. Johnson, who had transferred from the San Diego office to the New York office to help track down the sniper that had killed Senator Bainbridge, was monitoring and taping Junior's words and actions from a remote location in the jail, but he misinterpreted the prisoner's actions.

"The kid's irrational behavior indicates he might be at the breaking point," he said to his companion." They notified their superior in the New York office and she agreed it was time for another marathon interrogation of Junior McShane.

Agent Glitz knew the FBI was not monitoring the private telephone calls of its members, but the National Security Agency certainly was listening and storing the calls of everyone in the nation. She used a prepaid call card to notify Detective McShane of the upcoming interview. "2309 this is 2300. The FBI is going to grill 2308 again."

"Don't worry, 2300," he replied. "2308 will never betray us. 2308 is a chip off the old block and won't tell them a damned thing."

* * *

Moments later, Mike's phone rang again. "Dad please come and get us," Della cried.

"What's wrong, Della?"

"Me and Dawn got beat up, Dad," she tearfully said.

"What!" he shouted.

"There were four or five of them," she moaned. "'So your old man is a NYPD cop, huh?' they kept shouting."

It took Mike and Officer Borenstein less than 40 minutes to reach the campus police security office. Dawn had a bloody nose and some bruising, and Della was getting a black eye; their clothing was torn and they had been molested, but not raped.

"We think it was those punks from the Sigma Phi Tau Fraternity, Detective," the head of security told Mike. "The whole frat is members of Antifa. They were all wearing black jackets, pants, and facemasks, so our guy couldn't ID any of them. There's a kid over there named Bruce Harrison and he's a real troublemaker. Our patrolmen tried to intervene and now he's over at the hospital getting stitches in his head."

Mike left the girls with campus security and headed for the fraternity house with Officer Borenstein, but the place was empty.

"I promise you I'll handle this, Mike," Officer Borenstein said. "You take the patrol car and head back to the precinct and report the assault to the NYPD. I'll catch a ride with one of the guys that'll be meeting me here."

When the fraternity returned from one of their so-called protest meetings, they were horrified. They finally got a taste of their own medicine. Every room in the frat house was a wreck: all the beds had been turned over and stripped; every computer screen was smashed; curtains pulled down off the windows; books had been ripped apart; term papers torn into shreds; their clothing was torn apart and littered the bedroom floors; the refrigerator was turned over and all the food, beer cans, and beer bottles were smashed and scattered about the kitchen floor; the water faucets in the bathroom and kitchen had been turned on and the drains closed, and now the water was literally cascading down the stairs. Even their hidden cellphones, which they never carried to the demonstrations for fear of being identified, had been discovered and were smashed into several pieces.

Bruce Harrison, the frat house leader, picked up the phone to call the university's police, and that's when he discovered the direct line to campus security had been severed. He didn't know what else to do or who to call.

"Who is going to pay for all this?" the fraternity brothers wondered. They knew the college would not. The university's policy was that whatever happens in the frat house is the members' responsibility.

Dawn and Della dropped out of college. At this time it was impossible for a conservative to safely remain in most universities in the country, and anyway it was too far into the semester to register at another campus; maybe next year things would be better for conservatives on college grounds.

* * *

Things were strangely different now for Mike. He no longer had a passion for catching the sniper, because they were now on the same side, but he had to pretend he was just as enthusiastic as ever about it. He knew he could never get Gloria and Junior released, since they were federal prisoners and a NYPD detective has very little leverage with them. As he and the twins sat in the silence and loneliness of the home that had once been a haven of love and laughter, Mike pondered about the future of his family, his career, and the fate of the SDL.

*Who was the mole that had betrayed my family?* he wondered. *Was it someone in the SDL's New York cell? I am going to find out!*

He was so deep in thought that he missed part of the news broadcast on One America News:

"The president announced today that in spite of the four hundred billion dollar cut back in military spending, the rank and file military would receive an unprecedented 15 percent pay raise that will be partially funded by the drawdown of the number of Border Patrol and ICE agents ..."

A few moments later the president appeared on screen and remarked, "It's about time the guardians of our freedom and liberty were treated fairly. The raise in pay will be effective at the beginning of January."

"Members of the armed forces are delighted with the president's decision," the newscaster then continued, "and ..."

"Bingo." Mike shouted. "The Tri-Party is slowly tightening the noose around Lady Liberty's neck."

"In other breaking news," the telecast continued, "the NYPD has announced the arrest of drug kingpin Alvin Fornay. The sting operation netted more than three million dollars found hidden inside Mr. Fornay's box spring mattress in the master bedroom. He was released on twenty thousand dollars bail …"

"Twenty thousand dollars bail!" Mike shrieked. "That's peanuts to a drug king." But then he had an idea, and the next morning he called a friend who worked in one of the city's 77 precincts.

"You know, Mike," the officer said, "the money never appeared in our evidence locker. In fact, I called several other precincts, but no one knows who has custody of the cash."

Mike stopped at One Police Place and spoke to the police commissioner.

"The Feds took custody of the money," Robert Hereford softly said, "since they maintain the drugs were being sold across the state lines in Jersey and Pennsylvania."

It took several weeks, but Agent Sara Glitz confirmed Mike McShane's suspicions.

"Our source in Washington traced the money trail," Sara Glitz told him, "but it took a lot of digging. It was exchanged through several government agencies, including the FBI and the Department of Homeland Security before ending up in the coffers of the Tri-Party's National Headquarters in Washington, and that's not the only thing, Mike. It seems Alvin Fornay has disappeared. The Feds never put a monitoring device on him and of course he didn't have an American passport."

"So if a drug lord gets caught, the toady federal judges let him walk," Mike said. "The sad thing is that this is probably happening all across the US. That's another reason why Mayor Alvarez cut the funding from the NYPD budget. The Narcs lost a number of agents and arrests are down, allowing the New York Tri-Party's brass to virtually ensure that the kickbacks from the drug cartels will continue to fund their mandates, and is another major reason why the Tri-Party-controlled House is still refusing to fund the rest of the border wall. Felons like Fornay will go to another sanctuary city and start all over again, and the drugs will keep pouring across our southern border and the kickbacks will continue to swell the Tri-Party's coffers."

"Bingo," Agent Glitz replied, "and the attorney general is allowing the mayors of the sanctuary cities like Los Angeles, San Francisco, San Diego, Denver, New Orleans, Boston, Chicago, Baltimore, Philadelphia, and others to do the same thing without any investigation or charges being filed against certain drug dealers. However, if the dealers in the non-sanctuary cities are arrested and charged, they are remanded to federal custody, since the Feds claim they sold the drugs across state lines. When the dealers are released on cheap bail, they flee to a sanctuary state or city.

"In addition, the Tri-Party doesn't want to stop the flow of millions of illegals across the border because 98 percent of them will register as Tri-Party members. For every 770,000 people counted by the census, it means the Tri-Party usurps another seat of the 435 available in the House of Representatives. It is designed to help ensure the eventual emergence of a one-party system."

* * *

Mike McShane sipped a glass of wine to help subdue his anger as he again watched the late-night news.

*What the sanctuary city mayors are calling demonstrations are really riots,* he pondered. He watched a mob overturn and burn police cruisers and then the camera panned the flame-engulfed buildings in the business sections of the sanctuary cities. Other stores were being looted indiscriminately, while other thieves hammered away with tools, trying to open safes or cash registers. Other protestors stomped on and then burned the American flag, while others threw bricks or bottles at the hapless police force.

*They remind me of those wimps that did the same thing during the Vietnam War,* Mike mused, *and the socialist governors and mayors are still refusing to let the police do their sworn duty!*

The Antifa members continued to smash out storefront windows and then loot the merchandise, while the municipal police, garbed in riot gear, stood by and did nothing. Mike was an NYPD detective, who had sworn to protect and defend the citizens of New York, as the police in every American city swear to protect the citizens entrusted to their care.

*It was bad enough,* Mike mused, *when the leaders of the old Democratic Party encouraged their members to confront conservative public figures on the street, in their offices, trap them on elevators, get in their faces and run them and their families out of restaurants and other public places, or terrorize their wives, husbands, and children at their homes. But now, those Antifa mobs have really gotten out of hand and even the Tri-Party leaders can't control the looting anymore, since most of it is being done by ordinary citizens in the sanctuary cities.*

Mike was horrified. It was obvious the riots were planned nationwide violence events with political agendas, and he saw something else he never saw before. Instead of the Stars and Stripes, the rioters were waving flags with a blue background and had a single white star in the center that the broadcaster announced was the symbol of a single-party nation—the Tri-Party—and at every demonstration, Antifa members, the Boogaloo Bois, and the BLM radicals kept fervently chanting, "No more Trumpmeyer, no more wall, no more USA at all."

Mike recalled that a prior attorney general, Ericson Folder of the Ogama administration, encouraged his constituents to "kick their opponents when they are down," and Mike McShane placed his unfinished glass of wine on the coffee table, headed for the master bedroom, and began rummaging through the bottom drawer of his wife's dresser, where he now hid Jack Minzey's rewrite of David Greenfield's dialogue on The Second Civil War. He teared up at the sight of her clothing, but retrieved the copy of the discourse and read until he came to the paragraph:

When you hate each other but accept the election results, you have a country. When you stop accepting election results, you have a countdown to a civil war.

That's the crux of the problem, he pondered. The old Democratic Party never accepted the results of the 2016 election and tried to sabotage it. Trumpmeyer was and is a threat to them. Unlike the wimpy Ogama, who traveled the world bowing to Saudi princes and apologizing to every nation he visited for the humanitarian exploits of America's military heroes, Trumpmeyer—it turns out—is an ass-kicker and not an international ass-kisser like Ogama.

*Instead, President Trumpmeyer continually praised our men and women in uniform, who wrested Europe from the clutches of Nazism and prevented the further spread of Communism, and he thanked them for their service. President Trumpmeyer put America first, and by doing so he created millions of jobs, revived our sagging economy, strengthened the military, and halted the wildly unfair trade practices of errant nations. Even North Korea ceased the testing of its ICBM program. Then he forcefully dealt with the Wuhan virus.*

*But the old Democratic Party couldn't stand all of his accomplishments! They wanted their political power back, and cared little about the fate of our country, and now the Socialists, Progressives, and Liberals have seized control of the old Democratic Party and a good deal of the government.*

"Socialists will take by force what they can't win by legitimate elections or the rulings of those toady judges in the Ninth Circuit Court," Mike said aloud to the twins, Dawn and Della. "The Tri-Party advocates the use of force to gain or retain power just as the Socialists did in China, Cuba, Vietnam, Laos, and what is now happening in Venezuela. We are in a civil war, but most of America's private citizens don't recognize it or they're too frightened to face reality."

* * *

China was delighted with the turmoil the Tri-Party was wreaking in America, and continued drilling for oil in the South China Sea and other waters claimed by Vietnam, Indonesia, Brunei, and the Philippines for centuries, and no other nation was strong enough to stop them on their march to control the world's supply of oil.

Vladimir Putin, the President of Russia, was a former member of the Soviet Secret Police, the KGB, and harbored dreams of restoring the former glory of the empire once known as the Union of Soviet Socialist Republics since the day he took office. During President Ogama's inauguration, his armies boldly invaded and attacked Crimea in Ukraine. Then the Putin regime brazenly implanted the Russian flag on the floor of the Arctic Ocean, declaring that the land lying beneath the sea was a projection of Russia's land mass, and therefore the billions of barrels of oil pooled deep within the earth below the waters belonged to Mother Russia.

North Korea was now again testing the power of its atomic warhead ICBMs. The hatred between ISIS and the Taliban boiled over once more and launched a resurgence of hostilities in Afghanistan. With the aid of socialist Iran, ISIS again reared its ugly head in a multitude of Near East, Middle East, and Far Eastern countries, and the Ayatollah reiterated his oath to destroy Israel once and for all.

Throughout these ordeals, the socialist POTUS stood by and did nothing. He was too busy plotting to commandeer the liberty and freedom of the most democratic nation on the planet, and he would do so by force if necessary. Without a strong free world leader like Trumpmeyer, the entire world was now in chaos, and a weakened NATO was almost powerless against the socialist despots.

The United States was being weakened militarily, but because of its military build-up under President Trumpmeyer, it was still a lingering superpower in spite of the inner turmoil being instigated within its borders by the Tri-Party factions. However, the other free world leaders could only helplessly stand by and watch the unbelievable political events that were unfolding in America, and they held their collective breaths.

* * *

Later that evening, Detective McShane's phone rang: it was 2300. "A whistleblower in the DOJ leaked the report of the FBI's investigation of Jose Feliz's attempted murder of the POTUS. He tried to murder President Trumpmeyer of course, but he did not have any family members being vetted or prevented from entering the country as he claimed. It was all a lie. He told the FBI those factions favoring the left encouraged him to kill President Trumpmeyer since it was the only way they could defeat him!

"The leaker said Feliz volunteered to be the sacrificial lamb of the Tri-Party's plot to turn America into a socialist nation, and when and if it did, the new socialist president would eventually commute his sentence."

"So," Mike answered, "this open civil war began long before Senator Bainbridge was killed in San Ysidro."

"That is right, 2309," Sara Glitz answered, "the guerrilla warfare tactics began with the attempted murder of the POTUS during his 2020 reelection campaign, even though Special Counsel Mueller wrapped up his investigation and found no collusion with Russia by candidate and then President Trumpmeyer. The exposé of the phony dossier concocted by a foreign agent and paid for by Candidate Minton and the DNC with blessings of several high-ranking FBI leaders did nothing to quell their hatred.

"Even that impeachment farce, perpetrated by Speaker of the House Mandy Melosi and that liar, Senator Sniff of California, couldn't squash the popularity of the president, and it only served to fuel their loathing."

# CHAPTER 7

The Eagle watched the actions of Mandy Melosi, the socialist Speaker of the House, through the Scout Sniper daytime scope. Melosi was his target, but she was encased in a bulletproof glass enclosure, which the Eagle's informant didn't know about beforehand. The Eagle didn't have any armor-piercing cartridges to ensure penetration of the bulletproof glass. If he fired and the slug merely shattered the glass, he would never get another shot; it was better to wait for another opportunity.

*She and several other members of the defunct Democratic Party gave their blessing to the current violence by not condemning it, and thus exacerbated the undeclared Second American Civil War,* the Eagle thought, *and House Representative Jaxine Watters of the 43rd Congressional District, and Ericson Folder, a former attorney general of the Ogama administration, had encouraged the rebellion by encouraging Tri-Party members to openly confront Conservatives by getting in their faces, terrorizing their families, and kicking them while they were down. It was all preplanned to destroy the Trumpmeyer administration. The Tri-Party has retaken the House and the presidency, but it is still not satisfied.*

*It is an undeclared civil war,* the Eagle pondered, *because there was no formal declaration by the president and the Congress, and the outbreak of violence is not along geographic lines as it was in the first American Civil War. This violence is now occurring in every state of the union. But just as in the old civil war, brother is now fighting against brother, father against son, and women have joined the fray in unprecedented numbers, causing many mothers to oppose their daughters and for sisters to despise one another.*

*This Second Civil War is a conflict in which you don't know who the enemy is until the Antifa mobs form and openly clash with the American Eagle Militias, which is still occurring mostly within the boundaries of the sanctuary states and cities, but that is the only open conflict between bodies of combatants in this war. However, sniping and other insidious crimes are becoming more rampant in all the states.*

* * *

Nonetheless, President Garcia remained silent as the rioters continually smashed out storefronts and pilfered the merchandise within the red conservative states and the blue socialist states. It was just a matter of the Tri-Party keeping the chaos going until the socialist POTUS instilled enough fear in all the states to force them to agree to an Article V Convention that would make him an eternal president. But the destruction extended to black-owned businesses as well, and it soon became obvious the riots were going to continue even though the general election was long over and the socialists had scored significant victories.

*The president is waiting until millions more illegal immigrants pour across the open southern border,* Mike McShane thought as he watched FOX news and One America News, *and flock to the sanctuary states that guarantee them the right to vote. Untold thousands of rapists, murderers, drug runners, human traffickers, MS 13 gang recruits, Islamic fundamentalists, and innocent civilians are fanning out into every sanctuary state and city across the United States, and the depleted forces of Border Agents and ICE Agents are powerless to stop the flow.*

*Once they are settled in those states, the socialist POTUS knows their sheer numbers could influence two thirds of the state legislatures to request a Constitutional Convention to change our country to a Marxist nation and nullify the Second Amendment. Only the military is still powerful and large enough to quell the current violence and stop the illegal alien invasion, but President Garcia refuses to act, and soon the outbursts will be so large and numerous that even the military will not be able to contain them and more people on both sides will be injured or killed.*

* * *

*The sheer numbers of alien voters will assure the reign of socialism in the United States,* President Garcia thought as he gazed out the window in the Oval Office, *and I will be its first eternal president; it could be so easy! But I have to convene an Article V Convention to disarm the fools who keep hoping democracy will prevail. If I cannot disarm them by convening a Constitutional Convention, then I, as Commander In Chief of the armed forces, will have to resort to the use of military force to disarm them in spite of the Posse Comitatus Act of 1878 that forbids the use of military force to settle domestic policies!*

* * *

*It's like the war in Vietnam,* Mike McShane mused as he watched the insurrection in the sanctuary cities and states on TV, *you don't know who the enemy is until it's too late.* He was glad he was no longer a uniformed cop since they were now obvious targets in all the red and blue states.

*The Tri-Party won the presidency,* he thought, *and the House of Representatives—and now suddenly those two factions are the supreme law of the land; the Tri-Party no longer recognizes the legitimacy of the Senate or the rulings of the Supreme Court.*

Mike McShane read Mike Minzey's synopsis of David Greenfield's speech on civil war again and was amazed at the accuracy of its contents when he came to the part that read:

> Our system of government is based on the Constitution, but that's not the system that runs this country. The Democrat's system is that any part of government that it runs gets total and unlimited power over the country.
>
> If the Democrats are in the White House, then the president can do anything. And I mean anything. He can have his own amnesty for illegal aliens. He can fine you for not having health insurance. His power is unlimited. He's a dictator; whether it's federal or state, executive, legislative or

judiciary, the left moves power around to run the country. If it controls an institution, then that institution is suddenly the supreme power in the land. This is what I call a moving dictatorship.

At the next meeting of the Sons and Daughters of Liberty, Sara Glitz laid out the next planned phase of the Tri-Party.

"The POTUS plans to go on live national television and radio and demand an end to the violence now that millions and millions more illegal aliens are on American soil and registering as Tri-Party members in the heavily populated sanctuary states. That means only those few states will forever determine who our next president will be, no matter how the remainder of the country votes.

"His next intent is to call a Constitutional Convention— An Article V Convention—to ban the possession of firearms by American citizens by proclaiming it is necessary to protect our citizens in light of the multitude of recent injuries and deaths initiated by the unruly mobs of Antifa, the BLM radicals, and the Boogaloo Bois, but particularly the defensive measures taken by the conservative militias.

"It is the same ploy taken by Adolph Hitler," Sara Glitz said "to disarm the German people, which left the Jews, priests, mayors, and his political opponents totally defenseless.

"Of course, during the Article V Convention, President Garcia will try to decimate the Electoral College too," Sara Glitz continued to speak, "and elect the president by the popular vote only, now that millions of illegal aliens have registered with the Tri-Party. They also want to allow the chief executive to serve six consecutive terms. However, if he manages to change the country to a socialist government by force in the meantime, then changing the Constitution will be a moot point, since it will no longer be the supreme law of the land. At this point in time that is an unlikely event, but not impossible at some time in the future. They're covering their asses either way.

"Right now, POTUS needs three fourths of the state legislatures to ratify all three changes. If the Tri-Party succeeds in that endeavor, it will make those amendments the supreme law of the land—a communist land! He allegedly has the backing of two thirds of those state legislatures to convene a convention in light of the recent violence in all 50 states, but getting three fourths of them to ratify a constitutional change is going to be the next great challenge for the Tri-Party."

* * *

Sure enough two days later, the president appeared on national media and demanded an end to the violence, and as if by magic the ferocity of Antifa and other criminal groups in the sanctuary states and cities ceased, and an apprehensive peace reigned throughout the country. The next day POTUS made a public plea for American citizens to voluntarily surrender their guns to the nearest police station in the interest of peace and safety. Amazingly, many thousands of citizens throughout the country complied with his edict, but millions more did not.

Then POTUS closed the border and the influx of illegal aliens ceased. It was a meaningless peace gesture toward the conservative factions, since the Tri-Party now had enough registered illegal alien voters in the sanctuary states to compel the legislatures to call for a Constitutional Convention. Anyway, for many of the newest would-be migrants, the threats posed by the mayhem in the sanctuary states and cities was now as dreadful as the poverty and oppression they allegedly faced in the countries from which they were fleeing.

* * *

On the next visiting day, Mike McShane headed to Rikers Island to visit Gloria and Junior. The correction officer scanned the list and looked up at Mike. "I'm sorry, Detective, but we don't have any prisoners here by the name of Gloria McShane or Junior McShane."

"What do you mean there are no prisoners named McShane here," Mike screeched, "I've been visiting my wife and son here for the last month!"

"Sorry, Detective," the corrections officer replied, "but they are not incarcerated here."

Mike looked at him imploringly, and the jailer frowned for a moment, then turned his back to the camera monitoring the entry foyer as he stowed the visitor's logbook on the shelf behind the counter. Then, as he reached and opened the gun safe to retrieve Mike's pistol, the detective barely heard him whisper, "They moved the SDL prisoners late last night. Rumor has it they were transferred by executive order to those closed detention centers at the ports of entry along the southern border in order to split up the SDL cells, and because the president wants them tried in the Ninth District Circuit Court that's stacked with those toady liberal judges." Then he handed Mike his pistol.

Mike was stultified and just stood there dumbfounded.

*Some of those southern border detention centers are more than 1900 miles from New York City*, he pondered.

"Detective," the corrections officer loudly proclaimed, "I thought I made it clear. There are no prisoners by the name of McShane incarcerated here. Are you going to leave, or do I have to call security?"

Mike knew the man took a big chance in giving him the information about the prisoner transfers, and since the detective now had his back to the camera he gave the officer a tight-lipped smile and then said aloud, "No need for that officer." Then he turned and left.

* * *

Mike was angry and more determined than ever to find the mole who sent his wife and son to prison. Now they were confined on the other side of the country and he wondered, *Could the mole be a member of our cell, and if so, why weren't all the other cell members arrested?*

That night he worked into the wee hours of the morning, concocting a scenario designed to trap the spy, and at the next cell meeting he made a stunning announcement.

"It seems my wife Gloria has kept a list of all the members of the SDL in New York who she met. I found her record in our master bedroom closet in a green three-ring binder."

"That is a violation of the cell's rules," General Webb interjected.

"Oh, OK," Mike responded, "I'll destroy it as soon as I get home this evening."

Mike was planning to go home as soon as his shift was over. However, an anonymous caller tipped off the precinct that the wanted drug king, Alvin Fornay, was hiding at his brother's house in the Bronx, and Mike was assigned to the task force being sent to take him into custody. His plan to catch the mole had backfired.

*An operation like this takes time,* he pondered. *What if the mole breaks into my house while I'm pursuing the drug dealer and finds not only the green three- ring binder, but also Jack Minzey's treatise on civil war?* In a panic, he called Agent Glitz and told her what he had done.

"Don't worry, 2309," she answered. "We've got you covered."

* * *

The task force quietly ascended the stairs in the apartment building in the Bronx where Alvin Fornay was laying low; because he was a wanted fugitive, their guns were drawn, and several uniformed officers were covering the rear of the building.

Mike banged on the door and shouted, "This is the NYPD; open the door." He stepped to the side in case the fugitive fired through it, but there were no gun shots and no one answered his knock. He banged on the door again, and a moment later it opened and a frightened middle-aged woman panicked at the sight of their drawn guns and threw her hands up. They brushed past her as she flattened herself against the open door, but the only other person in the apartment was the woman's 85-year-old mother, who was confined to a wheel chair.

"It was a set-up!" Mike seethed. The other task force members merely nodded; they had been duped.

* * *

In the stillness of the night, a car pulled up to the curb in front of the McShane home, and a hooded figure in black clothing got out and scurried up the stairs. The perp inserted a pointed device into the lock and twisted it back and forth several times until he heard a distinct click.

The intruder knew Gloria and Junior were in federal custody, and that the twins stayed at a trusted friend's house while their dad was at work. Detective McShane was on an assignment, so there was nothing to fear. He turned on the flashlight in the darkened home and located the stairs, and moments later he entered the master bedroom. There on the top shelf in the bedroom closet he found the green three-ringed binder his compatriot had described and flipped through the pages. There were hundreds of names of SDL members listed. *It's a coup for the socialist movement*, the intruder joyfully mused.

He rummaged through Mike's highboy and then through Gloria's dresser drawers, spewing clothing on the floor before uncovering a jewelry box with several rings, necklaces, and a set of diamond earrings. It was more booty for the Tri-Party National Committee!

He found Gloria's papers and read the first few sentences of the Treatise on Civil War and thought, *aha, Detective McShane is also a member of the SDL!* Then he stuffed the pages into his rear pocket and scurried down the stairs, leaving the door ajar as he stepped on to the porch while looking up and down the street. There was no one on the sidewalk, but in the distance he spied a pair of headlights speeding toward him. The name *McShane* flashed through his mind, and he began running down the stairs.

From his hide amongst the leaves of the tree-lined street, the keen amber-eyed Eagle followed the perp's actions through his Starlight Scope as he came tearing down the porch stairs, and as his foot touched the bottom step the Eagle gently squeezed the trigger. The thief plunged headlong on to the sidewalk. Another figure rapidly emerged from the car and snapped up the green binder and then sped away just as Mike McShane pulled up to the curb.

In the radiance of the streetlights and the beams of his car's headlights, Mike immediately spotted a body lying on the sidewalk. When he pulled the burglar's hood off, he was shocked to see such a young face and the mortal head wound.

*My God*, Mike thought, *he's about Junior's age.*

There was no point feeling for a pulse. The detective searched the victim's pockets for an ID, but all he found were the stolen jewels and immediately recognized the unique diamond earrings he gave Gloria for their 20th anniversary. Then he found the treatise papers, and his pulse quickened.

"If the thief had gotten away and Agent Alan Johnson got hold of these papers, I would have been arrested; my prints are also all over them."

Mike then turned his head and spotted the open front door in the gleam of the subdued lighting and drew his pistol. He searched the house, but no one else was there.

Then he called in the crime, and less than five minutes later a patrol car pulled up. There were two officers and one of them was Kenneth Borenstein, a member of his SDL cell. The officer made a quick phone call, and when no one in the gathering crowd could hear him, he softly said to the detective, "2300 directs you to swear that you accosted the burglar as he exited your home."

Mike was horrified; he was about to issue a false report. He never did that during his entire 20-plus-year career in the NYPD! Then he remembered the oath he took with the SDL and his conversation with Father Ramon, *God, family, country, and city in that precedence. My family and my country first, and New York is a sanctuary city. This is a civil war—a guerrilla-style war—like the one I fought in 'Nam. If the FBI or the NYPD forensics ever discovers the spent bullet that killed the burglar and match it to the sniper's bullet, they will know I am a member of the SDL. But I took an oath with the SDL to defend my country and our form of government. But this is war and therefore I have no choice but to issue a false report.*

* * *

The next day the local papers ran this headline in large print:

## DETECTIVE KILLS ALLEGED BURGLAR

Detective Michael McShane of the NYPD's Central Park Precinct confronted a man who was burglarizing his home, and as the two men struggled for control of the officer's weapon the gun discharged, killing the alleged burglar. The victim had no credentials and police are asking the public for assistance to help identify the body. Detective McShane, the lead investigator in the unsuccessful attempt to end the sniper killings that have been plaguing the city, has been assigned desk duty while the Internal Affairs Bureau investigates the incident. Dr. Rita Simpson, the Chief Medical Examiner for the City of New York ..."

Two weeks later, Mike was restored to full duty. At the next SDL meeting, Mike asked Agent Glitz, "Why didn't the sniper also kill the man who seized the green binder that has the lists I copied from various pages of the New York City telephone directory?"

"Because," she replied, "we wanted the Bureau to spend hundreds of man hours running down that list and interrogating a lot of those people. They will use up time and resources that will keep them out of our hair for weeks."

"Well my charade proved one thing, Agent Glitz!" Mike said. "There is a mole in our cell. No one but our cell members knew about that phony list I made, so I guess my efforts didn't backfire after all."

"No it didn't, Detective, but if the mole is in our cell, how come we all aren't under arrest?"

Mike merely shrugged his shoulders. He was as stumped as she was.

"In the meantime, I'll update you when we learn the burglar's identity."

* * *

Two weeks later, Agent Glitz phoned Detective McShane: "This is 2300; we've identified the person who burglarized your home. He's was an 18-year-old kid by the name of Joshua Spencer, a staunch supporter of Rita Moreno, who has officially thrown her hat into the ring for a US Senate seat from New York."

"Joshua Spencer? I know that name," Mike answered.

"I thought you might, 2309. He was friends with 2308 and played sports at the place where 2306 works."

Mike knew 2308 was Junior's code name, and 2306 was Father Ramon, the pastor of St. Hedwig's parish.

"So," 2300 continued, "now we know why the government didn't arrest all our cell members. Apparently, 2308 and Josh Spencer were friends, and 2308 bragged about his affiliation with the SDL, but at the time 2308 didn't yet know the identities of the other cell members except for 2307. That's why only 2307 and 2308 were arrested."

Mike teared up at the number 2307—that was Gloria's code.

"OK, but how did they know about the green binder?" Mike asked.

"Good question, 2309," she replied. "I don't know. Maybe the FBI is shadowing us, hoping to learn the identity of other SDL cell members."

* * *

That evening, Detective McShane learned that COVID-19 was on the wane in all the states with the arrival of the warmer weather, and moments later he hit the record button on his remote to save a documentary being aired by one of his favorite news channels, One America News, depicting the everyday life of people living under the iron hand of the socialist government in Cuba. The host declared:

> The following documentary depicts the travels of a 77-year-old American man and his wife, who bicycled across Cuba for two weeks. It depicts what everyday life is like in a socialist nation.

> Cuba is a country where nothing works, including the people. Unemployment is 48% and of those who do work, eight out of every ten of them work for the government. Before heading to the western part of the island, we spent a night in Havana at the Riviera Classic, the finest hotel

at one time. It is 20 stories high with three elevators, but only one worked. Contrary to what I found in the rest of the country, my shower only had hot water. Turn the knobs all you want, but you only got hot, scalding water.

The stories about the old cars are quite true, but many of those cars are used to take tourists on tours of the city. Thirty American dollars gets you two hours in a 1952 Cadillac convertible and you can pile in as many people as you want. Old Chevys seem to be the most popular and a few are quite nicely restored. By restored, I mean they look good on the outside, but as our Cuban tour guide said, there would not be a V8 under the hood. The original engine had failed decades ago and with no parts to fix it, other means had to be found. Generally, that involved putting a 4-cylinder Russian-made diesel in and making the necessary changes to get it to fit and mate it up with an unknown transmission.

The country is still in the 19th century. Many people walk, but equally as many use horses, both to ride and pull carts. I saw wagons pulled by oxen on the highway. We traveled by motor coach, stayed in crude motels, and ate in restaurants— all owned by the government. Staying clean was a challenge. In the public restrooms, washing your hands was interesting. You need three things to wash your hands: water, soap, and a towel to dry them. Well, the towel was your shirt or pants because there never were any towels. In 1/3 of the toilets, there was no water, and in one case, there was a lady standing beside the sink with a bottle of water to pour over your hands. In an equal number of places, there was no soap.

If you thought not having soap and water in the restroom was a problem, imagine not having a toilet SEAT. Yep, no toilet seat and it's not just confined to public facilities. One of the hotel rooms we stayed in had no toilet seat, which was matched by the fact there was no toilet paper. In its place, somebody had carefully torn individual sheets of toilet paper from a roll and placed them on the back of the toilet.

Free healthcare and education is one of the things Castro brought with his revolution. The healthcare is generally limited to the bigger cities. Our guide told us that a taxi driver in Havana earned more in tips each day than a medical doctor earned in his salary in one month. Oh, and the doctor can be arrested and jailed if he attempts to treat people on the side for extra money.

Education is free, but the reality is that most people cannot afford to stay in school. Our tour guide was the exception. He completed college and got a master's degree in computer technology, but can't find a job in that field, so he conducts tours.

We visited a tobacco farm, where we had the opportunity to purchase genuine Cuban cigars for $3.25. The farm had been in this man's family for three generations, but only recently had the actual title been put back in his name. The government claimed it after the Revolution. After harvest, the government takes 90% of the tobacco, leaving the farmer with just 10% for his 'own personal use.' He chose to demonstrate how to hand roll a cigar, then sell it to tourists. I asked our guide if all farmers lost 90% of their crop to the government. His reply, 'Oh no, vegetable farmers only give up 60% of their crop.'

The roads looked like they had been carpet-bombed with huge potholes everywhere. One day I averaged just 4.5 MPH as I attempted to find bits of pavement between the holes in the road. In many cases, there was no road, just dirt, and when the trucks went past, we were engulfed in a storm of dust and exhaust fumes. A few of the trucks were leftover Russian military vehicles.

Personal transportation in the rural area was provided by stake-bodied trucks. People would stand by the side of the road and climb aboard when such a truck came by. The fare was around eight cents and you stood packed in the bed of the truck with several dozen other people.

Those on welfare receive $25 a month, plus a ration of beans, rice, and cooking oil. The money comes from the Cuban government, but the Russians provided the food. Each month, cargo ships dock with beans, rice, and cooking oil sent by Russia.

Glad I went, but have no desire to return. Cuba makes our inner cities look like paradise and the poverty is staggering. After two weeks abroad, we flew home, and I spent the night in a Hampton Inn at the Atlanta airport before catching an early-morning flight back to Seattle. I took the longest hot-water shower ever after having a cheeseburger, fries, and two gin & tonics for dinner. I was really glad to be back in the USA.

*Socialism,* Mike mused after watching the program, *means you eventually run out of other people's money by heavily taxing the wealthy individuals into poverty and businesses out of existence, thereby killing individual initiative and creativeness in order to support the entire nation. However, it also destroys your main sources of revenue.*

*Thus, there is no reason for individuals to think up and invent new products and ways to improve the means of production—which means hiring more workers—because the government owns and controls everything; that is the way a socialist government works. That is where the Tri-Party is leading us: to a one-party system—a communist form of government ruled by a dictator, like the government in Cuba.*

After he emptied his glass of wine, Mike McShane again picked up Gloria's copy of David Greenfield's discourse on America's Second Civil War as summarized by Jack Minzey paraphrasing the speech. He was finally going to finish reading it:

> What do sure odds of the Democrats rejecting the next Republican president really mean? It means they don't accept the results of any election that they don't win. It means they don't believe that transfers of power in this country are determined by elections. That's a civil war.

# CHAPTER 8

Mike McShane desperately wanted to see his wife and son, so he took two weeks' vacation. He peered out of the window as the plane skimmed above the waters of the Pacific Ocean before it landed at San Diego International airport. The last time he saw the Pacific was when he was on a TWA flight heading home from Vietnam.

The thought of seeing Gloria and Junior was exhilarating, and he hastened his pace as he headed toward a car rental service and then drove to the federal detention center at the San Ysidro Land Port of Entry just north of Tijuana, Mexico. He was disappointed and angry when he discovered the center was deserted, and a Border Patrol officer informed him Gloria and Junior had been moved to the federal detention center west of Anthem, Arizona.

"They're moving all the prisoners who are charged with sedition to various federal detention centers located in the Ninth Circuit Court's District to await trial," the officer said, "even though their alleged crimes were committed in different parts of the country. All the terrorist prisoners are considered flight risks so they are remanded to custody, and by keeping them within the Ninth Circuit Court's jurisdiction, the groveling federal prosecutors are certain any rulings on procedures will favor the government's case. It also makes defense counseling difficult, and the prisoners are unlikely to have any visitors."

A lengthy call to the prosecutor's office in San Diego verified that his family had indeed been moved to a federal detention facility west of Anthem, Arizona. The information left Mike more incensed than ever, intensifying his hatred of the Tri-Party. He flew into Phoenix Sky Harbor Airport and rented a car to drive to the federal detention center 25 miles north of the city, and that's when he learned that the prison housed male prisoners only.

A sympathetic detention officer revealed that Gloria was being held in the Federal Correctional Institution in Tucson, Arizona, a two-hour drive away. It had an administrative unit for both males and females awaiting trial. The frequency of visits at both prisons was determined by a point system, and since his family was new to the prison, their visiting hours were limited to one hour every other Sunday between the hours of eight thirty a.m. and three thirty p.m.

For the first time in his life, Detective Mike McShane began to feel the ugliness of an even more intense hatred engendered by this allegedly clandestine civil war that was predicated on the intentions of the wannabe socialist dictator who was currently occupying the White House.

*Amazingly,* Mike mused, a *Socialist was somehow elected president of this nation by an ignorant and apathetic constituency, many of whom are millennials whose "Everything For Free" mantra is banishing America's world-renowned reputation of being an economic powerhouse and the land of the free into the annals of history.*

* * *

"There are so many prisoners awaiting hearings here, Dad," Junior tearfully told him, "that my trial may not be scheduled for as long as two years."

The injustice caused Mike to tear up. He could see that his son had lost some weight and looked a few years older.

"Do you remember Josh Spencer?"

"Of course I do, Dad, he was one of my best friends in Saint Hedwig's School."

"He is the one who betrayed you and your mom."

Junior's mouth dropped open and then he asked, "Are you sure, Dad?"

"Yes."

"Well, he confided in me that he was working on Rita Moreno's Senatorial Campaign. I know she's a Democrat, but I didn't care. I told him mom and I were in the SDL, and if he wanted to he could visit me at the safe house in Yonkers."

Mike could see the anger rising in his son's eyes and facial features, as he tightly laced his fingers and mumbled, "When I get out of here, I am going to strangle that little son of a bitch."

It was the first time Mike ever heard Junior swear, and he had never threatened anyone, so the detective quickly answered, "You can't."

"Why not?"

"He's dead."

Again, Junior's jaw dropped and he leaned back in the chair. His voice softened, as did his facial expression, and he asked, "what happened."

For a brief moment, Mike sorrowfully thought of the time he held his own best friend as he was dying in Vietnam and thought, *death has a way of changing things, even anger and hatred.*

"I caught him burglarizing our home, and he tried to grab my gun and it went off, killing him instantly."

"Burglarizing our home?"

He could tell Junior was angry again, and he blurted out, "I'm glad that dirty double-crossing little bastard is dead."

But then he turned away. Mike knew he didn't mean it. *He's still a decent human being with feelings,* Mike thought, and he was glad. *But if he is going to survive here for two more years plus his eventual sentence, he'll probably become somewhat like a lot of other hardened criminals.*

"Time's up, McShane," the jailer shouted.

As Junior got out of the chair, Mike winked at him with his left eye and his son gave him a thumb up, and the defiant expression on Junior's face assured the detective that his son was enduring prison life.

*  *  *

But his visit with Gloria was another matter. She looked haggard and thin, and she seemed to have aged ten years. There were dark-colored bags under her eyes, and the prison policy was that all women prisoners would have their locks shorn so their hairline extended to no farther than the bottom of the neck. Her once long and beautiful raven-colored hair now looked almost as short as some men's hairstyles, and strands of gray were plainly visible among the darker tresses. It was heartbreaking for him to see her like that, and when she saw Mike on the other side of the glass partition, she began sobbing.

"They did a humiliating body cavity search when I first got here," she almost whispered. "Lieutenant Kilgore made me strip naked and had several male corrections officers standing nearby, stating they were a safety precaution in case I became violent. They made me lean up against the wall with my feet spread apart, while Kilgore probed my intimate body cavities with his fingers, and his thugs whistled and made jokes about what they would like to probe me with.

"Turns out many of the guards here are first generation immigrants and staunch supporters of President Garcia. They wouldn't let me wear any of my clothing when they escorted me to my cell, and deliberately took the long way around so we would pass through the male cell block."

Mike's heart was breaking because he couldn't do anything to ease her pain. He knew his warm and loving wife would never be the same. She was emotionally scarred for life! Kilgore had virtually raped and sodomized her. After his visit was over, Mike made a quick call to Agent Glitz at her home, using a disposable telephone calling card.

Mike told her about what happened to Agent 2307 in the prison, and 2300 replied, "I'm really sorry that happened to

Agent 2307, Agent 2309. We really admire her spunk. Of course, we can't restore her dignity, but we have a retaliatory crew that evens the score when one of our agents is sexually abused." She then verbally gave him a coded telephone number.

Several days later, at midnight, Lieutenant Kilgore was walking to his car at the end of his shift when out of the darkness a gruff voice commanded, "Kilgore, you make one sound and I'll blow your fucking head off."

He was accosted by two masked men brandishing pistols. They ushered him to a remote area of the employee parking lot, and soon he gasped and moaned with each successive blow. Hours later, an early morning prison worker found Kilgore's semi-conscious, beaten, and naked form sprawled face down on the hood of a car.

His badge, wallet, clothing, and credit cards were missing. He had two black eyes, cracked ribs, a broken nose, and his scrotum was bruised and swollen. Hospital personnel determined his recovery would take several months. Unfortunately, he would never know the reason why the predators beat him so severely, although he had his suspicions.

* * *

Mike thought about how ugly the situation with the Tri-Party members had become, but what the corrections officer did to his wife was an example of the hatred, disgust, and tyranny that civil wars invoke. He was glad Kilgore got his comeuppance, but his wife was scarred for life, and yet what happened to Kilgore made Mike certain of one thing. The

SDL was as tightly organized as Antifa had become, and when any member of either organization was hurt in any way, then sooner or later the enemy agent or agents were going to pay a terrible price!

* * *

After viewing and listening to the prison tapes, the warden and the FBI identified Detective Michael McShane as a person of interest in this horrible crime. However, the signature on the return portion of the car rental contract matched the one made by McShane when he arrived to pick up the car. The return flight time was ten p.m., an estimated two hours before Officer Kilgore's shift ended, and the airline employee working the gate for Mike's flight back to New York positively identified him from the FBI's photo gleaned from the prison tape.

"It was easy to remember him," the ticket agent told the FBI agent.

"He was that handsome NYPD detective who disclosed his .38 revolver was in his luggage and locked in a metal gun case, which made the weapon inaccessible during the flight; therefore, a National Law Enforcement Telecommunications System message to The Office of Law Enforcement/Federal Air Marshal Service wasn't necessary."

The Agent in Charge of the Tucson office was certain the assault on Lieutenant Kilgore was perpetrated by Detective McShane, but he couldn't prove it. He then called the New York office, and Agent Glitz assured him, "Agents from our office did indeed identify Detective Michael McShane when he alit from Flight 1520 from Phoenix at three thirty a.m. Our office and the NYPD have had him under surveillance for quite some time now," she told him, "ever since his wife and son were arrested for sedition. His two daughters are no longer in college, but they are above suspicion."

"Did you get anything from his phone tapes, Sara?"

"Nothing of interest," she replied.

Moments later, her phone rang again. This time it was Agent Johnson.

"We got a break in the SDL case, Agent Glitz," he said. "Rita Moreno gave the FBI a green binder that supposedly contains all the names of the SDL members in the city. The team will be on it by this afternoon. We dusted it for prints and guess what we found?"

"What?" Sara asked.

"You remember that kid Josh Spencer that Detective McShane killed?"

"Yeah."

"His and another set of prints were all over the green binder. Josh's mother and father said he was working on the Rita Moreno election campaign when he was killed. I spoke to some of Rita Moreno's staff," Agent Johnson continued, "and it seems this Spencer kid was in love with Rita Moreno and would do anything for her, even though she's 40 years old and he was 18.

"We also learned that another kid on her campaign by the name of Stan Garland was close friends with Josh Spencer, and we interrogated him. We discovered his prints were the other set on the binder, and he admitted he drove the car the night Josh Spencer was killed."

"How did they even know there was a binder with the list of SDL names in the first place?" Sara cleverly asked.

"Well, Stan Garland's stepfather is an NYPD cop named Kenneth Borenstein, and he is a conservative. Of course, Stan and his stepdad don't see eye to eye on anything. When Borenstein thought his stepson was asleep in his room, the kid overheard his stepfather tell his mother that Gloria McShane had compiled a list of SDL members."

*So,* Sara thought, *there is not a mole in our cell!*

"And so," Agent Johnson continued, "Stan Garland and Josh Spencer planned to sell the list to the Tri-Party National Committee for a lot of money, and then donate it to Moreno's campaign. But of course, when Josh was killed and Moreno learned from Stan Garland what he and Josh had done, she didn't want to have anything to do with the scheme.

"But here's the hook on this thing, Sara. Stan Garland swears Josh was killed before McShane even pulled up to the curb, and if we can prove that's true, we can nail McShane's ass to the wall for filing a false police report!"

"Well, if McShane didn't kill Josh Spencer, who did?"

"I'm willing to bet it was the sniper, Sara! And when we can find the slug that killed Josh Spencer and match it to the one that killed Senator Bainbridge, Mayor Alverez, and Pedro Rico, then we can positively link McShane directly to the sniper and the SDL." Sara knew Johnson was getting too close for comfort.

* * *

Moments later, Mike's phone rang: "This is 2300. You gotta find the slug that killed Josh Spencer! Agent Johnson is sending out a team in the morning to search for it. If they find it and match it to the bullet that killed the others, they are going to charge you with being a member of a subversive element, complicity in the murder of Josh Spencer, and covering it up by filing a false police report."

Mike was in a panic. The thought of the end of his career and years in prison raced through his mind, and he might never see Gloria or Junior or his two daughters ever again. He waited until the house lights in the neighborhood dimmed, and then searched the several front yards where he thought the bullet may have burrowed into the ground after passing through Josh Spencer's head. He used the flashlight sparingly, not wanting to attract attention.

He knew from the ME that Josh Spencer was five foot eight inches tall, and in his mind he conjured up the angle of the sniper's bullet that had passed through Josh Spencer's left temple and out the other side. He searched for hours with no luck and looked at his watch—it was four thirty a.m., and soon the FBI team would be scouring the area just north of his house, looking for the projectile.

Mike sat on the bottom step of his porch, sweating and stressed out at not knowing what else he could do. Time was running out, and as he anxiously gazed northward, he recalled the night Josh was killed. He remembered his headlights had picked up Josh's form lying on the sidewalk and a car speeding away, but something didn't seem right.

He thought about the scene for a long moment, and then he remembered the reflection of the beams from his headlights. It was something shiny he recalled, and then he remembered—it was the light rays reflecting off the windows of his neighbor's car that he sometimes left parked in his driveway overnight! Then he looked toward his neighbor's driveway, but the car wasn't there.

Mike tore up the stairs into his home, retrieved his police lock pick kit, and donned a pair of gloves. Minutes later, he inserted the pointed shaft into the side door of his neighbor's garage, praying it wasn't tied to the alarm system. It wasn't— and he quietly stepped into the garage. The flashlight batteries were growing dim, and he could barely make out the bullet hole in the car's back fender. He determined it entered the trunk, and there was no exit hole on the other side. He reached his hand under the dashboard and popped the trunk lid, and there on the far side was the spent bullet! He quickly stuck it into his pocket.

It had struck a toolbox and left it dented but did not penetrate the steel container. Mike was delighted but knew he was still in trouble. He quickly dashed back home and rummaged through his old jewelry box, and there amongst several old watches, tie tacks, his high school ring, and a few odd cuff links, he found it.

It was a spent slug from his Smith & Wesson .38 revolver that he kept as a memento of his pistol on qualification day at the

NYPD Police Academy more than 20 years ago. He returned to his neighbor's garage and found the batteries in the flashlight had died, and he silently felt along the edge of the car until his gloved hands felt the open trunk. He tossed the slug into the trunk and closed the lid. Then he made his way home again.

Less than an hour later, he sat behind the wheel of his car sipping coffee to stay alert before heading to his precinct office. As he backed out of his driveway and headed down the street, he glanced into his rearview mirror and saw several vehicles stop in front of his house; *it has to be the FBI,* he anxiously thought. *They must have been waiting for me to head into work.*

* * *

Later that morning, two FBI agents approached his desk as he was filling out some paperwork, and one identified himself as Agent Johnson.

"We need to see your .38 Smith & Wesson revolver, Detective McShane," the agent said.

"What for?" Mike asked.

"We found the slug that killed Josh Spencer," Agent Johnson gruffly said, "and we need to make certain it came from your S&W so we can wrap up the Spencer case." He didn't see a look of panic on the detective's face that he had hoped would betray his fear. Instead, he merely saw a smirk, although the detective looked rather fatigued.

"Oh, OK," Mike said, as he opened his desk drawer and remarked with a tight-lipped smile as he handed him the .38, "Be careful it's loaded."

Agent Johnson felt the slight and shot Mike a hardened look. It was insulting to tell an FBI agent to be careful about a weapon being loaded—they were trained to treat every gun that way.

*Smart ass*, the agent thought as he walked away with the revolver.

Later that night, Sara Glitz called Mike. "The FBI is not quite satisfied with the results of their findings," she told him. "The bullet they found didn't have the slightest trace of blood or any abrasions on it for a projectile that had recently passed through a man's skull and a steel fender. However, they admit the bullet was fired from your .38, but the trajectory of the shot is rather puzzling. You are right-handed and the slug passed through the left side of Josh Spencer's skull as it should have, but your hand must have been well above the victim's head when the gun went off to parallel the angle of the projectile. Thus, Joshua Spencer's death is still an open case as far as the FBI and NYPD are concerned."

* * *

*I never thought*, Mike ruminated, *things would get this bad in the good old USA, but I guess civil wars have a way of doing that and this one has only started!*

He realized his family and millions of others would never be the same, and couldn't help but remember that his son, Junior, was surviving his ordeal, but his attitude was slowly gravitating toward the brashness of a hardened criminal. Some of the jailed Conservatives were suffering from COVID-19, and although other criminals who had been convicted of some rather heinous crimes were being released, none of the SDL prisoners were set free. It was a melancholy situation for a dedicated husband and parent like Mike McShane.

* * *

Since the mainstream media was still ignoring the true cause of the crisis, the conservative American public consequently became slowly aware of the real reason such rampant violence was sweeping the country. Word amongst this group of citizens was being spread mostly by word of mouth, since only Fox News and One America News aired the truth about the chaos that was occurring sporadically across the country, but the worst violence was still happening in the sanctuary states and cities.

*There are no armies opposing one another,* Mike thought. *It's guerilla warfare with sniping, stabbings, raping, choking, or the ambushing of known Socialists and Conservatives. After confronting known Conservatives and anyone else they do not recognize, the masked hordes retreat like cockroaches back into the woodwork, while the local police stand idly by and are restrained from interfering by the orders of the sanctuary state governors or municipal mayors. However, the police are ordered to immediately respond to the presence of American Eagle Militias that are attempting to protect the rights of Conservatives to peacefully assemble.*

* * *

Although the militias were armed and in most instances they outnumbered the municipal police, they refused to confront the law enforcement officers in any manner since they were not viewed as the enemy. Many officers had resigned because of the danger and / or due to being restricted from doing their sworn duty to protect and defend the public, and the sanctuary cities were actually defunding their police departments, which dangerously thinned the Long Blue Line. Still, there was no investigation or inquiry into the riots by the Department of Justice, although mounting pressure from the right forced Attorney General Vincent de Leon to finally promise he would "look into the matter."

In the meantime, the destruction of public and private property continued unabated, as stores were torched and ransacked, and iconic images depicting likenesses of American history figures were destroyed or defaced, including the statues of Christopher Columbus, a black regiment from Massachusetts that fought in the American Civil War, Ulysses Simpson Grant, Andrew Jackson, General Robert E. Lee, and others. Then the crowd began targeting the statues of Jesus Christ. All this destruction occurred with the Tri-Party's blessings as they smirked and maintained their silence on the matter since the uprisings kept slowly nudging the nation toward anarchy and a one-party system.

It was the new Tri-Party and yet it was, in reality, that same old Democratic Party that enforced slavery in the pre-Civil War Confederacy, gave birth to the Ku Klux Klan, imposed the Jim Crow Laws, segregated educational facilities, and beat or lynched any black man who had the audacity to look at, talk to, or marry a white woman. All that injustice had changed over the decades, and yet the leader of the BLM swore his organization would not stop participating in the destruction of the current American way of life and its political culture until it was all torn down and a new nation emerged from the ashes. It would no longer be a nation where freedom and liberty reigned under the auspices of a Constitution for more than 244 years. It would be a new nation ruled by a despotic few: a socialist nation—a communist nation!

* * *

Then the Black Lives Matter movement posted a website that showed all the donations made to it were being funneled into the coffers of the Tri-Party. In reality, the Tri Party was the old Democratic Party that no longer espoused the philosophy of Franklin Delano Roosevelt, Harry S. Truman, John F. Kennedy, and Lyndon Baines Johnson, who signed the historic civil rights legislation into law. Those political figures would be abhorred by the current philosophy of the Tri-Party. The old Democratic Party was the party those Democratic leaders had rebuilt into the status of an iconic American political institution in the aftermath of the American Civil War. But that image no longer existed.

* * *

It was a Friday afternoon and the Eagle was clutching his valise and hiding behind the open doorway leading to the inside of the mosque. The muezzin had called the faithful to prayers (adhan) and soon all would lay in prostration to God (sujud) facing Kaaba in Mecca, Saudi Arabia, and chanting their daily prayers (salat).

When the worshippers knelt on their prayer rugs laying on the musalla, and their foreheads, nose, hands, knees, and toes all touched the mat at the same time in prostration to God, the Eagle quietly and quickly slipped inside the mosque and mounted the counter-clockwise staircase inside the minaret.

He stopped at the gallery from where the muezzin had called everyone to prayers and couldn't help but admire the ornate muqarnas that transitioned the walls to the magnificent, ornamental vaulted dome. The muqarnas were intricate and beautiful; they had to be, for in the Muslim faith they represent the universe created by God.

The minaret was the highest tower around for miles as it was intended to be, and provided a great view of the stadium. The Eagle poked the M16 through the ornate opening at the end of the gallery and peered through the Scout Sniper daytime scope. He scanned the crowd of red MAGA hats, but he didn't see anything suspicious. There were thousands of supporters packed into the stadium wearing those hats that paid tribute to former President Trumpmeyer and his efforts to "Make America Great Again." Such gatherings still incensed the left, even though former President Ronald J. Trumpmeyer had been nearly stabbed to death by one of their own kind and a socialist president now occupied the White House.

Then the Eagle focused his attention on the stands and the stage. He was almost 600 meters from the podium where Mike Fence, the 2024 Republican presidential candidate, was scheduled to speak. His life had been threatened many times on nearly every aspect of social media. However, no arrests were ever made, and since everyone entering the stadium was being scanned for weapons with a "magic wand," the Eagle presumed that security inside the stadium was adequate enough to keep the Republican candidate safe. However, the high-ranking spy in the Garcia administration warned of a threat to his life, and the Sons and Daughters of Liberty sent their anonymous sniper to counteract the threat.

The Eagle began scanning for possible sniper hides outside that oval arena, but only one structure in particular caught his attention. It was a church steeple towering above the houses in a residential neighborhood that the Eagle estimated was less than 380 meters from the podium that was situated on a raised stage inside the coliseum.

The church was much closer to the stadium than the minaret. He adjusted the scope to its ultimate focus and began scanning the structure and something immediately roused his curiosity. It was sticking out from in between the louvered panels of the church steeple and was barely perceptible even through the powerful optical lens of the SSDS. It was centered in the wooden louvered panel facing the stadium and protruded about four inches.

The louvers protected the bell tower from the elements, but the spacing between them allowed the clanging of the church bells to be heard for miles around. Then the Eagle centered the reticle on the center of the panel facing the mosque, but all he saw were the wooden slats and nothing more. Whatever was sticking out through the panel facing the stadium made it look slightly different from the panel facing the mosque. When he shifted the scope back to the panel facing the stadium, he was amazed to see the object had disappeared, but now he realized what it was. It was the muzzle of a rifle!

That sniper had obviously focused the scope lens on the podium and was now awaiting the arrival of the Republican presidential candidate. But the steeple was out of the 550-meter maximum effective range of his M16 rifle. The Eagle had estimated the sniper was less than 400 meters from the podium, well within the effective range of most high-powered rifles. There was no time or place to get into a different position to get a better shot at the would-be assassin!

The Eagle glanced at his watch. Mike Fence was scheduled to speak in about half an hour, which would give the party elite time to warm up the partisan crowd. The Eagle and the enemy sniper patiently waited, but the candidate was more than an hour late and the Eagle knew he was in trouble since he was going to be missed at work.

Then the candidate suddenly appeared on stage and the Eagle could hear the rousing cheers emanating from the enthusiastic crowd. He swung the rifle around and focused it on the panel facing the stadium. What looked like the muzzle of a rifle was again protruding from in between the louvers, and the Eagle knew he had to do something no sniper ever wants to do.

The target was out of the 550-meter maximum effective range of the M16, but within its maximum range of 3600 meters. He would have to judge the distance by eye, and he raised the scope several clicks and then one click left, hoping the bullet would at least wound the would-be slayer.

That familiar old phrase lingered in his psyche for a brief moment and then the Eagle felt the kick and saw the louver above the muzzle splinter; the shot looked a bit high and he took the slack out of the trigger, ready to fire again, when suddenly the muzzle tilted skywards for a brief instant and then disappeared back inside the steeple. His mission was now accomplished, and it was time to get the hell out of there.

The Eagle bounded down the stairs and mingled with the Muslim faithful as they were exiting the mosque from Friday afternoon sunset prayers, and although he looked like every other Muslim exiting the mosque, the Imam gave him a puzzled look when he spotted the valise that one of his faithful was carrying.

When he got back to work, the Eagle lied to his superior and feigned a case of nausea and vomiting and said he had gone to the nearest urgent care center, too distraught to notify anyone. He was reprimanded severely by his boss for alarming his compatriots when he failed to show up for the planned dinner, and he promised it would never happen again. Later, he would retrieve the valise from the dumpster behind the building where he had hidden it. The Republican candidate would never know he was in danger or ever meet the man who had saved his life!

Several days later, Detective Mike McShane got a call

from Agent Sara Glitz. It was an official call to Detective McShane in his office so there was no need to talk in code.

"When a church deacon ascended the steps to ring the church bells for Sunday services," she said, "he discovered a decomposing body in the steeple. When I and the NYPD officer got to the scene, I recognized the body of Stan Garland from the photo Agent Johnson sent me. It was the kid who drove the car on the night you encountered Josh Spencer burglarizing your home. We also learned Stan Garland was an avowed socialist like Rita Moreno, the Tri-Party senatorial candidate from New York, and that he also fraternized with members of Antifa.

"Near as we can figure, he allegedly was planning to kill the Republican presidential candidate Mike Fence, who was holding a political rally at Veteran's Memorial Coliseum not far from the Lutheran church where the body was discovered. The ME consulted a forensic entomologist and she calculated the date of death from the stage of development of the insect infestation. In this case it was the blowfly, and it was attracted to the corpse by the body fluids and gases.

"'It usually lays its eggs within two days of death,' the entomologist told the medical examiner.

"They determined from the pupal stage that Stan Garland was killed approximately on the same date the Republican rally was being held in the coliseum," Sara told Mike. "We found a Soviet-made AK-47 on the floor near the body. He was shot once and the bullet that killed him was fired from the same gun that killed Senator Bainbridge, Mayor Alvarez, and Pedro Rico."

"But how did the sniper know Stan Garland was allegedly planning to kill the Republican presidential candidate at the rally?"

"Obviously, Mike," she replied triumphantly, "SDL now has spies that have infiltrated Antifa and the Boogaloo Bois, just as they have spies in the American Eagle Militias."

* * *

Agent Johnson read Agent Glitz's report of the shooting, stared at her for a long moment, and said, "This thing is getting way out of hand, Sara. It's time for the Bureau to go public with what we know."

The disclosure made nationally breaking news, and forced the government to recognize the national uprising, and that the left's fake news cohorts failed to air the fact that a multitude of such crimes were being committed all across the United States by those who favored the Socialists, as well as those who supported the conservative viewpoint.

The Second American Civil War was now a legally-recognized problem, a guerilla style of warfare where the enemy was unseen and unknown except during the open clashes between the American Eagle Militias and Antifa, and increasingly the Boogaloo Bois and the Black Lives Matter radicals.

That news finally compelled the socialist POTUS to dispatch military units to quell the periodic eruptions in the sanctuary cities and states to protect all citizens from looting, beatings, rapes, and murder. But a military presence only exacerbated the situation for the anarchistic Antifa, the Socialists' enforcement arm that viewed the military as supporting a strong central government. This is something they loathed and soon the military peacekeeping soldiers also came under fire by Antifa, while the Boogaloo Bois concentrated their fire on the federal, state, and municipal police. Both schemes were big mistakes!

The actions of the terrorists caused the federal police, the military, and the municipal police forces to form a loose alliance with the American Eagle Militias, which were composed of grassroot American citizens who had the same aims as law enforcement had of protecting the citizens of the United States. This informal axis was strictly forbidden by POTUS. He needed to retain the absolute loyalty of the military if he were to disarm the American public after convening a Constitutional Convention to negate the Second Amendment, nullify the Electoral College, and extend his presidency for five more consecutive terms. In fact, he hoped the military and the American Eagle Militias would clash.

He fired general after general and admiral after admiral, but none would betray that sacred piece of cloth with its 50 stars and 13 stripes. He even thought of hiring foreign generals. However, he knew the Senate would never confirm them, and he was beginning to realize the rank and file military would never follow their orders no matter how hard he tried to bribe them with pay and benefits. Those military men and women were patriots who took a great deal of pride in serving their beloved country and its "melting pot" of citizens.

President Garcia had never served in the American military and didn't know there wasn't a damned thing he could do about the friendships forged between the men and women who served a common cause and that they quickly become brothers and sisters in combat. They were putting their lives on the line for their country every day, and soon that loose coalition between the military; the federal, state, and municipal police; and the American Eagle Militias developed into an iron-clad alliance.

That coalition was widely portrayed in the mass news media as a threat with the intent of driving a wedge between the military and the American Eagle Militias. However, the scheme backfired. The well-armed American populace suddenly became sick and tired of the violence, the looting, rapes, beatings, and murder. They wanted a return to normalcy, and they now stood openly and solidly behind the forces of law and order, and soon swelled the ranks of the American Eagle Militias until they outnumbered the number of men in uniform.

When the news reached the ears of the amber-eyed Eagle, he knew he had accomplished his mission; all of patriotic America from the grassroots level on up was now united against the common foes: socialism, the anarchistic Antifa, the extremely far-right Boogaloo Bois and the radical offshoot of BLM, all of whom were in bed with the Tri-Party.

* * *

In spite of the violence and the COVID-19 pandemic, socialism continued to rear its ugly head in the United States with the inception of the Medicare for All Program. The bill had been introduced in the Tri-Party-controlled House without reference to its cost. Republican swampers in the Senate sided with the Tri-Party House members. The GOP senators were fearful of the alleged growing popularity of socialized medicine as depicted in the main news media, and those swampers feared not being reelected if they did not support the bill.

The legislation was immediately signed into law by President Garcia, and the national debt soared from 24 trillion dollars to 55 trillion dollars overnight. It was a major political victory for the Socialists, but the real turmoil in America was just beginning.

The word spread like wildfire around the world about how the nation that offered the best medical care in history was now offering free medical care to all—no one could be denied coverage—and you could pick any hospital or physician you so desired! An avalanche of humanity, composed of illegal immigrants from nearly every other nation on Earth, once again migrated toward the southern American border.

In the sanctuary cities and states, the membership of illegal aliens had swelled the ranks of the Tri-Party, and the state legislatures were calling for an Article V Convention to guarantee a crystallization of a one-party system in the United States that would last for the remainder of the century, and perhaps beyond, since the country could be ruled by an eternal president elected by the heavily populated voting bloc of the blue states!

* * *

"The Medicare for All Program sponsored by the Tri-Party," Dr. Rita Simone said as she opened the discussion at the next SDL session, "and its promise of free medical care for all, caused another flood of undocumented aliens to bring with them many of the diseases that had almost been wiped out in the United States. The outbreak of these epidemics has paralyzed many hospitals, and the overcrowded conditions have only worsened the outbreak.

"The staffs are overworked and medicines are in short supply since an angry China stymied the export of all medical supplies. People are sleeping on gurneys in the hallways or on the floor in the hospitals or wherever there is a space available, and many of the caretakers are also falling ill. Some hospitals are forced to shut down for extended periods, and doctors in private practice are inundated with patients as well."

"The fabric of Middle America is being shredded," Mike said, "since the full impact of the millions of unskilled migrants is being felt now that they have entered the labor market in every state in the union, working for cheaper wages or getting paid under the table. The result is a drastic drop in the tax base.

"Cheap labor is again replacing millions more of the lower middle- and upper middle-class Americans," he told the cell members. "The once booming economy fostered by the Trumpmeyer administration absorbed the initial shock, but many of the unemployed native-born Americans, who are being replaced by the so-called undocumented workers, are being forced to live on whatever savings they have. Taxes under socialist programs have increased exponentially, forcing millions of small businesses out of existence, causing masses of more employees to be laid off, swelling the rolls of the social programs, and driving millions of American citizens and non-citizens alike to seek relief.

"Those who have IRAs are using the funds to meet expenses and paying the severe tax penalty for early withdrawal, and those who were still employed are paying the 70 percent tax rate needed to fund the new Medicare for All Program."

"Unemployment applications for the millions of middle- and lower-class Americans also ballooned with the advent of their job losses," Police Commissioner Hereford chimed in. "They were replaced by the horde of illegal immigrants whose numbers now far exceed the declining number of work openings. The economic chaos is causing the sanctuary states to beg for federal aid, but the national government is too awash in debt to bail them out again!"

"The unemployed Americans and illegals are known as the Gray Class," Sara Glitz spoke up, "and their ranks swelled with the former members from the upper, lower, and middle class, as higher prices and spiraling taxes have lowered demands for goods and services. This has radically slowed American spending, and sales of new automobiles have slumped drastically and pulled the demand for steel and aluminum down with it."

"In three years' time, the number of Americans traveling to vacation spots or celebrating the holidays came to a near halt with the COVID-19 pandemic," General Webb said, "but the economy was recovering. However, the cost of social programs is causing the economy to flounder again, and multimillion-dollar airliners sit idly on the tarmacs while the pilots and air crews drift into the Gray Class.

"This drop in air travel and automobile trips greatly lowered the demand for fossil fuels, so refineries drastically cut production, and no new oil wells are being drilled in Alaska, Texas, and other oil-producing states; the active operating wells are drastically cutting production—even Canada is feeling the pinch."

"Yeah, heating oil production has slowed dramatically," Officer Borenstein added, "and Americans and families in other countries have lowered their thermostats and bundled up to keep warm; even though heating fuel prices had decreased somewhat, prices are still relatively high worldwide, especially in Europe. China and Russia are becoming increasingly at odds with one another and have mobilized their militaries as they struggle to determine which of their currencies will replace the American dollar as the world's petro currency."

"The demand for new shoes and clothing diminished as the economic chaos no longer made fashion as important as putting food on the table or paying the electric bill," Dr. Simone spoke up again, "and as the nation abandons the notions of style and flair, the textile mills and leather goods manufacturers are following suit. Many of those factories have laid off more workers or closed their doors forever.

"The railroads and truckers feel the pinch too, as requests for the myriad number of retail products and services they deliver fell off sharply with the decrease in wages and increased unemployment, and the miners feel the squeeze as the need for coal and iron ore used in the steel mills is no longer in great demand.

"Americans by the millions sought to join the military "Dr. Simone continued, "whose pay increase made the armed forces alluring, but the drastic decrease in defense spending stalled the demand for any great number of new recruits and the number of reenlistments is at an all-time high. America is well on its way to becoming a second-rate military power, much to the delight of China that now boasts of having the world's largest economy and the planet's most powerful military. Iran, North Korea, Syria, and a slew of smaller Middle Eastern countries are again threatening the existence of Israel.

"And now China, sensing the demise of the United States as a world power, has dumped trillions of American T-Bills on the open market. However, their strategy is backfiring; no other country can afford to buy them! They brought those T-bills with the money gleaned from the terrific trade imbalance between the US and China before President Trumpmeyer imposed his tariffs on them to even the score.

"The New York Stock Exchange averages have plunged, as Americans and foreign investors keep selling off their portfolios—at staggering losses—to put food on the table, gas in their cars, and to pay property taxes. The slumping of the New York Stock Exchange brought down with it the economies of every other nation on Earth! America's fate is a financial pandemic that is scourging the entire financial world, including that of China."

* * *

"But the world's biggest nightmare has only begun," Sara Glitz said. "With the sudden influx of millions more of illegal aliens, the demand for food and its price has skyrocketed. That sudden increase of many millions more mouths to feed cannot be supported or sustained by the American farmer. Additional crops take months to grow and be harvested, and it takes several years to raise beef stock and hogs, and chickens and turkeys disappear off the shelves before a new supply arrives in stores.

"In the more and more rural areas across the nation, farmers awake to find their fields stripped of a great deal of their crops, and orchardists are discovering their fruit trees are being picked nearly clean. Only a few fruits in the uppermost branches remain intact. It eventually forced the farmers and orchardists to arm themselves and stand guard to keep from being robbed blind.

"Unfortunately, American food exports have come to a virtual standstill, causing more unemployment at the shipping docks and hunger and unrest in the foreign nations that depend upon American farmers for foodstuffs.

"Unions all across the country are in an uproar but to no avail, and more charitable organizations and the government are compelled to open additional food kitchens in every large city in every state in the nation. Long bread lines have formed as tens of thousands of American families, untold millions of illegal aliens, their children, their parents, single parents with children, and minors unaccompanied by an adult stand in line for hours hoping for a meal before the charitable kitchens and the government-subsidized eateries run out of food. Many of the poor despondents look like war-time orphans from scenes in the films of post-World War II European countries. Men are unshaven, women have unkempt hair, and many are garbed in clothing they would have donated to charity, thrown out, or used as rags just three short years ago.

"Fist fights break out when these hungry citizens and non-citizens alike push and shove each other to get closer to the head of the line, and the sanctuary state governors and city mayors are suddenly allowing their police forces to do their jobs to keep order. But the shorthanded and underfunded law enforcement men and women must don riot gear when the huge numbers of the hungry masses clash and things gets out of hand; occasionally, paramedics are called to treat the injured.

"Criminal activity of every other sort keeps soaring, and undermanned police forces struggle to contain the bedlam. Already, thousands of illegals have begun drifting back toward their native lands, but millions more no longer have the energy or wherewithal to make the long trek. Actually, the situation there is no better than in the US!"

"Oddly enough, the mutinies between those who wear MAGA hats and the socialist terror organizations of the Tri-

Party first slowed and have ceased weeks ago," Mike McShane chimed in. "Hunger has a way of doing that to a nation in the throes of an undeclared civil war, where no one is happy, few remain healthy, and most go to bed hungry every night.

"The United States is still in the throes of a Marxist grip even though there are no longer enough state legislatures supporting the Tri-Party's wish to convene an Article V Convention. Their struggle to change the American democratic form of government to a socialist regime, annul the Second Amendment, and demolish the Electoral College no longer has support at the state level; at the moment, hunger is the most important problem.

"The USA is now much like the chaos still festering in Venezuela, where food and medical care are scarce, even though that country has one of the largest oil reserves in the world. Its Socialist dictator, Nicholas Maduro, is to blame.

"The mayors of many sanctuary cities are now offering the undocumented aliens a free year's rent if they could find housing in a non-sanctuary city, and thus many illegal aliens migrated to other states where their sheer numbers caused the same havoc they inflicted on New York City, Los Angeles, Chicago, San Francisco, Minneapolis, Boston, and Baltimore.

"After the tax base plummeted and food prices soared," Mike McShane continued speaking, "the citizens in the sanctuary cities and states that once welcomed the illegal aliens now look upon them with an unabated hatred, and they now abhor that influx of humanity which is virtually decimating the food supply, clogging the courts, and overrunning the schools, hospitals, the job market, and vying with American citizens for private and public housing.

"There were very few new private houses being built, which is causing a shortage of private homes, and no public housing is being built anywhere in the country; there is not enough tax money to pay for them, and very few native Americans in the middle class could afford to pay cash or mortgage the tens of thousands of repossessed homes that are coming on the market. Many building contractors went out of business too with the housing bust, and thousands of small banks and many branches of the larger ones have been forced to close their doors forever.

"The schools can no longer hire teachers who can bridge the language gap, and the demand for free school lunches has skyrocketed in proportion to the millions of new mouths to feed.

"The death toll amongst the elderly rose to staggering proportions as greedy pharmaceutical companies refused to lower their drug prices until it was too late. Much of their profits dropped in proportion to the elderly death rate. The United States once offered the greatest medical care in the world, but now it was relegated to a mere shadow of that former image. Even being as proficient as it once was, those American medical professionals could not sustain the impact of millions of new patients who suddenly thrust themselves into the number of existing hospital wards, emergency rooms, clinics, and outpatient health care centers."

* * *

Every major nation on Earth now looked at America's dwindling military might with disdain. The United States was no longer the world's policeman, brokering peace with its military prowess and economic power. It now stood at a socio-economic crossroads, and millions of the illegals strived to return to their native lands or move closer to their families where they thought they would be better off during this worldwide crisis. But the US government couldn't afford to pay their airfares or to buy bus tickets to shuttle them back to the southern border. These millions of illegal aliens were now stuck in the mess they helped to create!

# CHAPTER 9

There was a series of eerie uprisings in socialist countries around the world where economic conditions had also worsened and the COVID-19 pandemic was still spreading fear. Dictators tightened their strangleholds on the compliant populations in China, Russia, Vietnam, Laos, and Cuba by use of military force and arrests. The shaky axis formed by those countries was stunned even further when OPEC lowered its prices and contemplated the conquest of the world by controlling the price and supply of oil and natural gas.

By military threats, China had usurped the waters claimed by Vietnam, the Philippines, Indonesia, and Brunei for centuries. It was still drilling in those waters to extract the billions of gallons of oil pooled beneath the sea beds to counter the Saudi threat, and with the turmoil roiling the United States, the free world was powerless to stop it.

Russia was doing the same thing in the Arctic Ocean and the Beaufort Sea north of Alaska, claiming that the sea beds lying beneath those bodies of water were an extension of its landmass, and therefore the oil lying beneath those depths belonged to Mother Russia.

Vietnam, once America's archenemy, now begged for American military assistance. However, the drawdown of US military might, under the auspices of a socialist president, was slowly approaching the influence of a third-rate power.

There was a silence in the halls of Congress, signaling a stagnant economy in a nation whose once vigorous citizens drove a bustling business environment and enjoyed a lust for life made affordable by that economic bedrock known as capitalism. There individuals were free from government interference that stymies the new ideas that foster new inventions and create new industries and the growth of the ancillary businesses associated with them. Socialist programs in America were destroying the life of a country that was once viewed as the Garden of Eden.

* * *

Under such dire economic conditions, there was little support by the state legislatures to convene an Article V Convention to change the United States from a constitutional republic to a socialist nation, where the government controls all means of production and the distribution of all the goods and services of the economy. The country instead was perplexed by a plethora of socialist programs that produced the same dire symptoms that eventually ail all communist nations.

The United States of America, once the brightest political star the world has ever known, had lost its luster. Hordes of immigrants no longer tried to sneak across the southern border into the US; drug smugglers caught breaching the border wall and the open desert fell to an all-time low, since few addicts could afford the cost of addictive drugs and thousands succumbed to an agonizing death; MS-13 gang members no longer saw any real criminal opportunities in America now; new waves of human traffickers almost ceased to prosper; and the number of suspected terrorists apprehended at the ports of entry was virtually nil. The weight of debt had caused the American nation to collapse, just as it devastated the communist empire once known as the Union of Soviet Socialist Republics!

* * *

It had been more than three months since Mike McShane visited Gloria and Junior, but it was the fall and the airlines again were shut down following a new recurrence of the Wuhan virus. Therefore, he motored across the country for five days heading to Arizona. He soon learned gas was not as available as it once was, and when he did find a service station, he sometimes had to wait in line for hours to fill the tank or get a limited number of gallons available at the pumps; gas was being rationed along with food, medicines, and clothing.

Sometimes he drove for hundreds of miles without seeing another car or a truck, and food was even harder to find, especially in the Midwestern states. In one small town off the interstate, the store's owner told him truck deliveries were sporadic all along the route. Mike wisely bought some canned vegetables and meats, and the purchase proved to be his sole source of nourishment for the last three days of the five-day trip. So many hotels and motels were out of business that for four of the five nights, he was forced to sleep in his car. But that was OK; he was going to see Gloria and Junior very soon.

He decided to roll into Tucson to see his wife first, and when he entered the visitor's lounge of the Federal Correctional Institution, he identified himself and told the corrections officer why he was there. The corrections officer, an older gentleman with the name tag Richard Ryan, looked at a document lying on the counter in front of him, and he shot Mike a horrified look. "I'm sorry, Detective McShane, didn't you get the Warden's letter?"

"What letter?" Mike asked.

"It was sent out about a week ago, Detective. Your wife is gravely ill."

"What's wrong with her?" Mike asked, as he suddenly choked with emotion.

"She came down with COVID-19, Detective McShane. She's in the prison hospital ward."

"I want to see her," Mike almost shouted.

"Yes of course, Detective. I'll call the hospital staff and make the arrangements."

She was on a ventilator, but when he tapped on the glass window to let her know he was there for her, she didn't respond.

"She can't hear you," a strange voice said from somewhere behind him.

It was a man wearing personal protective equipment: gloves, a face mask, a face shield, an air-purifying respirator, and a gown.

"I'm Doctor McGregor," he said, "and as the warden explained in his letter, we had been treating her with hydroxychloroquine and doses of azithromycin, but there was no improvement. We've had her on intravenous remdesivir for 24 hours now, hoping that works."

"My God," Mike blurted out, "she got Guillain-Barré syndrome five years ago from a mosquito bite when we were on vacation in the Caribbean. Doctor Price said it may have weakened her immune system."

Doctor McGregor merely nodded and replied, "I got her medical records from Doctor Price." Then suddenly he looked past Mike and dashed back into the ward. Mike turned to see what startled the doctor and was horrified to see several nurses feverishly working on Gloria's prostrate form. He saw the doctor press the defibrillator to Gloria's bare chest and watched in horror as her body arched from the electrical charge. Mike had to cover his eyes with his hands; he couldn't take anymore.

After the third unsuccessful try, Doctor McGregor knew any further attempts would be useless. When Mike looked again, they had already covered Gloria's body with a sheet and the nurses were wheeling her out of the ward. Rules concerning a prisoner who died of COVID-19 in the federal prison system demanded they be interred as soon as possible.

Mike covered his eyes again and slid down the wall on to his knees. He had just lost the most precious treasure he ever had and he openly wept as he knelt there. "I never got to tell her I loved her or hold her or kiss her or say goodbye," he mumbled to himself.

Sometime later, a sympathetic Doctor McGregor helped him to his feet and escorted him to the veranda overlooking the prison cemetery. There would be no funeral with family and friends in attendance; no flowers; not a decent coffin to lay her to eternal rest in the spartan prison cemetery. After the prison chaplain finished saying a few prayers over her grave, Mike watched the pallbearers lower her into the freshly-dug grave site. As per prison rules, only a simple headstone with her name and date of birth and death would mark her final resting place.

As he stood on the veranda, Doctor McGregor again approached him. "This could all have been averted," he said. "I warned the government about how contagious this disease is and that we may not be able to contain it in such closed- in quarters. We released bank robbers, rapists, child predators, murderers, scammers, and white-collar thieves. But President Garcia steadfastly refused to release any federal prisoners who belonged to any so-called terrorist group."

*How am I ever going to tell the kids?* Mike pondered.

Then it hit him: *what about Junior!*

He scurried back to the desk in the visitors' lounge and the same corrections officer who checked him in called the prison where Junior was incarcerated, and Mike prayed his young age would protect his son.

"Your son was transferred to the Federal Correctional Institution on 45th Street in Phoenix," the officer told Mike, "since the Anthem facility doesn't have much of a medical department."

At the sound of his words and the look on his face, Mike McShane knew his son was also dead, and he shuttered for a moment when his warm and caring soul abruptly turned as stone cold as the heart of the most hardened criminal. *My wife, my children, my country, and my city are the things I love more than anyone or anything else in the world. That socialist bastard has murdered them,* he pondered, *and now he and others like him are striving to destroy my country and the freedom and happiness of millions of others like us who once enjoyed life thanks to the American military might that had protected us from the hell of Armageddon!* The hatred was an ugly feeling, but Mike McShane, a devout family man, an NYPD detective extraordinaire, and a combat veteran, who had served his country in peace and war, no longer had a reason to care about anything else except the twins.

*It is a well-known fact,* Mike reasoned, *that by keeping the SDL members in close proximity to one another in prison that COVID-19 would spread rapidly and many would die; my wife and son were deliberately murdered!*

Mike McShane's fate had been forged by forces beyond his control, and now he knew his destiny was to somehow help rid his country of the evil known as socialism and kill the wicked socialist fanatic that helped cause it all: President Luther Garcia.

* * *

The 2024 elections were fast approaching in the United States, and out of the chaos, poverty, shock, and disillusionment, the disenchanted American nation gasped and then grasped at the sole ray of hope shining through a bleak and darkened nation, and the rest of the free world anxiously awaited the news after learning that the former President of the United States, Ronald J. Trumpmeyer, had once again thrown his hat into the political arena! The news sent Antifa, the radical element of the BLM, and the Boogaloo Bois into a frenzy!

* * *

But by killing prominent Tri-Party members, the Eagle had angered Antifa, the BLM radicals, and the Boogaloo Bois, and forced them to show their ugly hands by again openly attacking their political opponents at conservative rallies, on the streets, in the churches, schools, and in their homes. But those actions in turn had given birth to the American Eagle Militias. Those patriotic everyday Americans now outnumbered the Tri-Party, Antifa, the Boogaloo Bois, and the BLM radical element by the millions.

It was time for the American public to strike back at the Tri-Party's goals that were again destroying what was left of America's liberty and freedom, and that of her allies. That ability to fight back was only made possible thanks to the saving grace of the Second Amendment of the Constitution of the United States!

There was no other way to broker the peace; the enemy was unwilling to negotiate unless all levels of government were disbanded, the police forces defunded, and the American military establishment was to be relegated to that of a third-world power. The Socialist was able to initiate the change because they were armed, but the rest of America is also armed unlike those in the Socialist's world. The time had come to kill this cancer that was eating away at the fabric of American life, and it had become obvious to the public that if the everyday American patriot didn't do the job, it would never get done—and if they didn't act soon, the greatest country in the history of the world would soon disappear forever.

The military veterans and retirees had organized the American Eagle Militias into platoons, companies, battalions, and regiments, each with its own commander—and now in every major city, town, and burg across the country, the factory workers, who still had jobs, turned off their machines; the mechanics in the repair shops dropped their tools; the farmer left his fields; chefs left food cooking on the grills or baking in the ovens; soccer moms left their children in the care of relatives; and the millions of the unemployed rushed to America's defense.

Americans of all colors, races, and creeds who loved their country and the American way of life had agonized over its future and that of their children and families for too long. They now joined the endless procession of young and old Americans heading to assembly areas all across the sanctuary states, carrying a variety of arms and ammunition of every caliber and description. They were everyday Americans and they were angry; they had enough.

* * *

President Garcia ordered the military to destroy the American Eagle Militias, and every aspect of the fake mass media flocked to the points of potential conflict to record the slaughter.

However, trained officers and the rank and file soldiers know the provisos of the Constitution, and were aware that it was not up to them, and never was up to them, to determine the political fate of the nation. That prerogative belonged to the civilian population and every military man and woman was subject to them, and when the ground combat units arrived on the fields in the blue states, they beheld the masses of armed men and women wearing citizen's clothing.

In those ranks were their brothers and sisters, cousins, aunts, uncles, and even their mothers and fathers who composed the army of civilians on both sides that they were now facing. Consequently, the American infantrymen and their commanders refused to engage or fire upon the citizens they loved and were sworn to protect, and they remained loyal to their Constitution and their country, not a wannabe despot. Besides, those two groups had formed an iron-clad bond during prior encounters with the socialist radicals.

As per the Posse Comitatus Act, the military units remained in formation and saluted the flag as they watched the marching patriots carry the stars and stripes into battle against the sham nation known to the radicals as Capitol Hill Organized Protest or CHOP that had seized a section of Seattle with the consent of the city's Democratic mayor, who labeled the secession as a love festival. Later, they would march into Portland, Oregon and do the same to that so-called autonomous nation that sprang up in the heart of the city.

The American Eagles made easy targets for the young Antifa, BLM radicals, and Boogaloo insurgents who were protected behind barricades. The patriots were in the open, and as the first Eagle casualties fell, the rioters let out a rousing cheer as they watched the colors fall. However, youth and inexperience cannot match the courage and know-how of grizzled old veterans that had garnered their chutzpah in battle, and one of them picked up the fallen national ensign with one hand and urged his compatriots forward with the other.

The firing continued and the media cameras were rolling, and to the delighted of the film crews it looked as though the renegades were winning, but many of the insurgents who dwelled in that lawless community were dazed by their drunkenness and drug-crazed minds; they were useless soldiers, although many others were not high.

Then suddenly a volley from 150 rifles of a flanking American Eagle Militia company drowned out every other sound on the battlefield. The frontal assault by the American Eagle Militia was a distraction so that the enveloping company could position itself in the streets to the right side of the insurgent's line and arrive undetected, abruptly making the defensive barriers a useless form of protection.

The incessant crossfire from the front and flank continued and soon the thinning ranks of the rebel line began dropping to the ground next to their dead and wounded, covering the back of their heads with their hands in unconditional surrender. On cue, the ambushing militia ceased fire, and the attacking Eagles in the frontal assault unit swarmed over and around the barriers.

The armed rebels in the rear formation discarded their weapons and didn't stop running until they reached the only safe place outside of CHOP: the streets of downtown Seattle. Their demands for anarchy, their arrogance, hatred, and everything-for-free attitude meant nothing in combat. An eerie silence briefly ensued, but soon the screams and cries from both sides of the line could be clearly heard on the TV and video cameras.

It was all over in less than a half hour, and soon the stars and stripes fluttered on a makeshift pole in the early evening breeze in the former self-proclaimed independent nation once known as CHAZ that the rebels had later renamed CHOP. The militants who ran did not return, and now the US military did take action as their medics and corpsmen fanned out on both sides of the barriers to treat the casualties, while the remainder of their medical teams began setting up hospital tents so their doctors and nurses could attend to the most seriously wounded.

Pain medications and bandages were in short supply, just as they were when the colonists clashed with British troops during the American Revolution more than 244 years ago. Men and women, who only moments ago were shooting at one another, now lay side by side on the ground, withering in pain or numbed with shock. Their hatred of one another vanished as they waited their turn to be carried into surgery tents on stretchers or race away in ambulances with screaming sirens and flashing lights, heading toward the nearest civilian emergency rooms.

The dead on both sides were laid side by side depending on whether they died in the frontal assault or behind the improvised barriers so graves registration personnel could identify the remains as accurately as possible. Some bodies on both sides lay putrefying among the ruins until the next day until more help arrived from the federal government and distraught family members arrived to help identify the remains.

It was not a pretty sight to see military personnel in gowns, gloves, and masks lifting the decaying bodies onto stretchers, and then putting them onto deuce and a half trucks to be driven to makeshift graves dug for the bodies that remained unclaimed. Many Americans, who lost a son or daughter or other loved ones who had patronized either side, could not bear to watch the horror.

For those corpses that could be identified, their families would have to wait until their loved one arrived home in a closed casket, and after the funeral they would be buried in a place and manner of their family's choosing. Unfortunately, a number of Antifa, the Boogaloo Bois, and BLM radicals would be granted the identity in death that they so fanatically desired in life; their headstones would be forever marked as UNKNOWN.

More than 250 million Americans saw that live horrible carnage of combat and later its dreadful aftermath, and soon thereafter they also watched other youths abandoning the other so-called autonomous nations that had sprung up in the heart of nearly every large American sanctuary city; the open fighting was over!

The members of Antifa, the Boogaloo Bois, and the radical elements of the BLM movement who survived would move on and shroud themselves in the underground like so many other criminal elements. An uneasy peace now reigned in this economically challenged and chaotic nation.

* * *

Sister Mary Theresa, Order of Saint Francis, stood silently in the Mother Superior's office and listened as Sister Clarinda read the letter. "The Archbishop of the Los Angeles diocese has specifically asked for you by name," she read. "He desperately needs your help out there.

"Your return will be effective as soon as possible. You have been of great service here and we shall miss you, but the LA diocese is in such despair and is in dire need of help. The bishop sent you plane tickets with the letter that says a limo will pick you up tomorrow morning at four a.m. to take you to JFK for your early-morning flight to LA. Somehow, you bumped another passenger and the airline gave you priority status." *I don't know how the archbishop managed to do that*, the Mother Superior thought. *Seats on every flight are at a premium.*

"Yes, Mother Superior," the young novitiate obediently answered, then she was dismissed. That evening at dinner, Sister Mary Theresa said her goodbyes to the nuns she came to know so well, and then she immediately retired to her room to begin packing for her cross-country journey and to get a good night's sleep before arising before the dawn. She would be gone before the sunbeams shattered the night sky and her vestal friends were still asleep in the nunnery.

* * *

Sister Mary Theresa looked out the window of her modest convent room and up at the cross above Saint Hedwig's Church for the last time, and she smiled. She had done her best. Then she slowly removed the black veil with the white lining from her head; the wimple covering her face, neck, and chin; and the large white collar that modestly hid the outline of her breasts. The novitiate placed these garments on the bed, and then unabashedly stripped naked.

Being a transgender woman was the perfect masquerade!

It completely fooled the nuns in the Franciscan Order and the NYPD a number of times when he nonchalantly walked away in his disguise after snuffing out his intended targets. They never suspected a Catholic nun of being the deadly sniper! The Eagle had remained in top physical condition by doing the same variety of calisthenics he did when he was active military after supposedly retiring to his room each evening.

He felt his full breasts, knowing they would completely disappear within several months' time, along with the smooth layer of fat that had widened his hips. Even his rough beard had turned into wisps of thin, sparse blond hairs that he easily shaved off each morning to avoid detection.

Estrogen supplements had caused those changes by suppressing his testosterone production. But the antiandrogens were his biggest concern. Those 5a-Reductase inhibitors had sapped a bit of his energy and caused his erectile dysfunction. He apprehensively looked down at his penis and testicles, and hoped there wasn't any permanent damage. He hadn't had an erection in almost two years. The Air Force doctor that concocted his disguise also warned him his ejaculate might also be reduced or he might have dry orgasms for the rest of his life. But he was willing to risk all that for his country, as he had imperiled his life on the battlefield many times as an Air Commando during his tours in Iraq and Afghanistan.

The amber-eyed Eagle donned the blue suit hidden beneath a habit hanging in the closet, and uncoiled the rope he used to rappel from his third-floor room when he was on a nighttime mission and had to leave the convent undetected. When he returned, he climbed back up the rope to his private quarters. Before and after a daytime mission, he merely strode in and out of the convent in his nun's garb, carrying the gray leather valise, and no one was ever the wiser.

Then he pulled the gray valise from the back of the closet before moving the bed next to his third-floor window. He would just loop the rope around the bed post, instead of tying it like he used to, so he could pull it down with him since he would no longer have to climb back up. His mission was accomplished, and he thought about what he and other patriots had done as he continued packing.

The SDL appreciated the cooperation of the Archbishop of Los Angeles, and the two fake letters he sent to the Mother Superior at St. Hedwig's; one got him admitted as a member of the Order of Saint Francis, and the other was used to get him out of the convent. It was all part of a ruse to protect and defend America's constitutional government.

His role of targeting the Tri-Party elite as a member of the Sons and Daughters of Liberty had angered the entire left and exposed the true political intent of Antifa, the BLM radicals, and the Boogaloo Bois. His sniper actions ignited an FBI investigation, which also led to exposing Antifa's murderous role in killing low-level grassroots Conservatives across the nation. The exposé also convinced the general public that the Garcia administration was complicit in those murders by forbidding the Justice Department to initiate an investigation, even though he was aware the terrorist organizations were crossing state lines to commit homicide. Also, the silence of the fake news media that helped to cover up the slayings by depicting them as being a result of gang violence really ticked the public off.

The Eagle knew if the Conservatives swept the 2024 elections, the government would open an investigation and the appointment of a special counsel to determine what charges would be brought against Antifa, the BLM radicals, and the Boogaloo Bois for their criminal activities at conservative rallies and targeting individual Republican Party elites. Charges were also pending against those three terrorist organizations for inciting and prolonging the violent demonstrations that rocked the nation in pretense of honoring George Floyd's memory. He was a black man, a lifelong criminal, that was murdered by a member of the Minneapolis Police Department.

All those radical actions by the left incited ordinary citizens to form the American Eagle Militias to protect themselves from the enforcement arm of the Tri-Party and the tyranny of a budding socialist nation. The militias were composed of grassroots Americans and their ranks now numbered in the millions, and they were still on the move!

*Yes*, the Eagle triumphantly mused, *we have accomplished the mission! But I and the Sons and Daughters of Liberty couldn't have done so without the help and info given to us by Pablo Ramirez, the Vice President of the United States. The information that this army veteran and native Texan passed on to the SDL was absolutely critical to the mission. We did not want to do things this way, but pitting violent countermeasures against violent offenders was the only way we could have saved the nation.*

At eight that evening, the Eagle wound the rope around the bedpost once, then lowered the valise and the suitcase into the darkness until the rope slackened and he knew the gear was on the ground. Then he grabbed both strands of the looped rope and slithered to the ground, pulled the rope down, picked up the valise and the suitcase, and walked to the curb where his SDL cell leader, FBI Agent Sara Glitz, was waiting for him in the rented limo.

# CHAPTER 10

On his last month of service in the NYPD, Mike McShane was accorded the privilege of handing out the diplomas to the latest graduating class at the Police Academy. The top honor graduate ascended the stage and shook hands with Mayor Phil Sandoval and then with Police Commissioner Robert Hereford. He shook Mike's hand rather firmly and returned the detective's smile, and when he accepted his diploma, his amber eyes betrayed his delight at being among the newest members of the NYPD.

Mike was somewhat startled. He had seen that appealing smile before, but for the life of him he couldn't remember where or when he met the honor graduate, and it bugged him. The next morning, he peered at his computer screen and looked at the officer's record. His name was Ronald Schaffer, and he had served several tours of duty in Iraq and Afghanistan as a sniper with Air Force Special Tactics before entering the Police Academy. Therefore, it came as no surprise to Mike when the Academy's records showed the recruit proved to be an expert shot with both the rifle and the pistol, and his physical prowess was the envy of his Academy classmates.

Mike McShane knew General Webb, the highest-ranking commander in the Sons and Daughters of Liberty, had also served as the commanding general of the Air Commandos for a number of years. But he couldn't make any connection between the two.

Several weeks later, Mike and his twin daughters sat watching television in the loneliness of their home that once rang with the happiness and laughter of a typical American family. Mike and the twins missed Gloria and Junior so much that they sometimes teared up at the thought of their lost loved ones. The scene was repeated in thousands of American homes whose family members served on either side of the horrible civil war.

There came a sharp rap on the door. It was a manly knock, and the sound echoed throughout the room and startled the twins, but when Mike opened the door clutching his .38, no one was there. He stepped out on the porch and spied a gray valise.

He was hesitant. *Is someone setting me up?* he thought. There were sporadic killings still going on across the country as one person or group felt they had to even the score with someone; this could persist for years, Mike knew.

Then he remembered Gloria's retort when he told her she could be arrested for being a member of the Sons and Daughters of Liberty: "So be it!"

She and his son had given their lives for what they believed in and as he defiantly grabbed the valise, he said, "So be it!" But there wasn't any explosion. He brushed past the twins, who were still watching TV, and Dawn asked, "Who was it, Dad?"

"Just some guy selling magazines," he instantly replied as he kept on walking.

He retired to the master bedroom and closed the door in case something happened when he opened the luggage. There was no fire or explosion when he opened it, but he was amazed at what he found inside. It was an M16 rifle with a Scout Sniper daytime scope mounted on the Picatinny rail. There was also a Starlight Scope, two loaded 20-round magazines, and several boxes of 5.56mm rounds.

Mike was very curious, and the next day took the rifle to the NYPD shooting range and fired off several rounds. Later, a ballistic tech confirmed the bullet was fired from the same weapon that had killed Senator Bainbridge, Mayor Alverez, Pedro Rico, Hilary Minton, and several other lesser-known individuals. But the civil war was unofficially over, and the New York sniper hunt was now a cold case—all the evidence had been relegated to the evidence locker.

Several weeks later, Detective Mike McShane formally retired from the NYPD with over 21 years of service. The twins, Dawn and Della, felt safe at home alone now, and Mike was packing his bags and heading for a vacation in Florida. His cell phone rang and a muffled voice said, "President Garcia is going to be in Alexandria, Virginia on …"

* * *

Socialist President Luther Garcia was now running for reelection because he was unable to get two thirds of the state legislatures or two thirds of the Congress to convene an Article V Convention to nullify the Second Amendment, a proviso to elect the president by popular vote only, abolish the Electoral College, and a stipulation which would allow the president to serve for six consecutive terms—a virtual dictator.

The polls were appalling and made it obvious to President Garcia and the Tri-Party that he would not be reelected, and he watched the novel furniture being unloaded at his new home in Alexandria, Virginia. The house and its furnishings were secretly paid for with funds from the Tri-Party coffers, courtesy of the drug dealer, Alvin Fornay.

The president was the head of the Tri-Party, which was still a powerful position in American politics, and he knew he would still have millions of followers if and when he was defeated for reelection. He was being encouraged by the Tri-Party National Committee to consider running for the Senate seat vacated in Virginia if he didn't win reelection as president. The party guaranteed him the liberal governor would appoint him to serve out the remainder of the current socialist Senator's term since he had fled to China in light of his alleged corruption and probable indictment if a new administration were sworn in next year. Virginia had replaced New York and California as the seat of Socialism in America, so President Garcia's appointment and later his election to the Senate would amount to a shoo-in.

But the eye now peering through the Scout Sniper daytime scope was that of the blue-eyed Eagle. The socialist president had caused the deaths of his wife and son, and the Eagle knew he would never love another woman for as long as he lived; *the best part of my life is over forever,* he mused. A string of familiar phrases suddenly pulsed through his psyche: *tighten your grip; watch the reticle; wait for the kick.*

The FBI determined the bullet that killed the president was fired from the same rifle that killed the other elites in the Tri-Party and a plethora of drug dealers, and the FBI immediately reopened the case of the New York sniper killings.

*Strangely,* Mike pondered, *I don't feel any sense of satisfaction by killing the socialist president because it didn't resurrect the love of my life or my son. Actually, I don't feel anything inside anymore.* As he sat on a beach chair in Miami, Florida, he watched the waves pounding the shoreline while contemplating his future.

*My life is over,* he mused, *but my new will is made out; the twins will get the house and everything else I own; they'll do OK.*

He made up his mind as he thought about his service in Vietnam, when death was all around him and his fellow Marines every day, and he felt a sudden sense of solace. *My social life may be over,* he pondered, *but I am going to die a hero too just as my best friend did defending the line in the Phu Bai perimeter. I pledged to protect the people of my beloved city, and I am going to spend the rest of my life doing just that by ridding it of the scum that is slowly destroying the lives of so many citizens that live in the greatest city in the world.* At the thought of going back on the job, he suddenly felt a sense of well-being.

*I feel as though my life has meaning again,* he triumphantly mused!

* * *

He was a retired NYPD detective and knew who his targets were and where they frequented the city. Several MS-13 gang members were mysteriously killed recently, along with a number of looters who had continued to smash out store windows. The amount of die-hard leftist protestors, who were still surreptitiously throwing rocks or other projectiles at the police, dwindled with each pull of the trigger. Sometimes, the blue-eyed Eagle picked off several targets in quick succession, and with each shot a familiar phrase rang through his psyche—tighten your grip; watch the reticle; wait for the kick—and when he felt the kick and saw each evil target fall, he felt elated. *I'm back on the job I love,* he pondered, *protecting the people of the City of New York and members of the NYPD.* But in his mind, he knew his patriotic mission could not last forever, but he didn't care because when he left this godforsaken world, he would be rejoining the love of his life forever!

* * *

Several months had passed by, and the city's drug dealers were now extremely wary of the sniper in light of their rising death toll. It seemed uncanny, but the sniper somehow knew who, when, and where the drug dealers would appear. Several drug runners of Pedro Rico's old gang had already been killed, and a certain young blonde addict impatiently watched the dealer as he anxiously looked up and down the street as the money and then the drugs changed hands.

The blue-eyed Eagle felt the kick!

Not a sound was heard, but she screamed and ran when Alvin Fornay's blood splattered on her face and clothing. Then Mike McShane went scurrying down the stairs as fast as he dared when suddenly he was face to face with a police officer mounting the steps, holding his drawn pistol. *I guess it is my time to die,* the retired detective mused, *but I'm gonna die like a man, just as my best friend did in Vietnam.*

The two men stared at one another for a brief moment, and Mike felt a wrenching feeling in his gut when he recognized Ronald Schaffer, the top graduate in the Police Academy's graduating class that Mike helped officiate.

The amber-eyed police officer immediately recognized the man and the gray valise he was carrying, and looking directly into the blazing orbs of the blue-eyed Eagle he said, "Too bad about President Garcia."

At that moment, Mike realized who tipped him off about the vulnerability of the former socialist president. Then the patrolman gave the detective a wide grin, and suddenly Mike remembered Sister Theresa's smiling face!

"Be careful, Detective McShane," the officer said as he continued his run up the stairwell, "the New York sniper just killed another drug dealer."

Mike was stunned. He didn't know how the rookie police officer pulled it off, but the amber-eyed Eagle had fooled everyone; he had been disguised as a Catholic nun when he was the New York sniper. The retired detective was so flabbergasted that he forgot where he was for a moment because he was feeling ecstatic at finally solving the mystery of the sniper's identity. Then he continued dashing down the stairs and into the safety of the subway entrance.

* * *

Several months later, Mayor Sandoval proudly announced that the mystery of the New York sniper had finally been solved.

"One of our rookie patrolmen encountered and killed a retired police detective by the name of Mike McShane," Mayor Sandoval announced, "as he was attempting to flee the scene after shooting another drug dealer. A test bullet fired from the M16 he was carrying matched the ones that killed President Luther Garcia, Senator Nathan Bainbridge, New York Mayor Francisco Alverez, a number of drug dealers and their henchmen, and half a dozen MS-13 gang members.

"Detective McShane had once been the lead investigator in the New York sniper case," the mayor lamented, "no wonder the NYPD couldn't catch him. However, another mystery of the New York sniper has cropped up. The FBI knows he had an accomplice, since our records prove that Detective McShane was on duty in the city at the time of Senator Bainbridge's murder in Arizona. Therefore, the New York sniper case is still open."

The liberal news media triumphantly announced Detective McShane's demise, but the adverse newscast backfired when native New Yorkers learned of his identity and vigilante exploits. Of course, there would be no official funeral for the cop-turned-killer, but the city's top government officials and the socialist city council members couldn't stop the thousands of off-duty uniformed policemen from attending his wake, and then saluting the veteran's flag-draped casket as the funeral procession passed by. The open warfare was over, but policemen all across the nation were still being sporadically murdered in the nation's sanctuary cities, and the officers knew his actions had save the lives of some of New York's finest. The warning of the mayor and the city council concerning the spread of COVID-19 didn't intimidate the hordes of citizens who gathered along the route of his motorcade, carrying signs that read, "We Love You, Mike" and waving American flags.

Mike McShane got his wish. He would forever be remembered as an unsung hero to the citizens of the city he loved and so gallantly served. The recent civil war had that kind of effect on the nation's psyche. The native New Yorkers knew the Tri-Party administration that was running the city government was corrupt, and what Detective McShane did was the only way to get rid of the filth that still prowled the city's streets, poisoning the minds and bodies of future generations of Americans with their illicit drugs, gang murders, and human trafficking.

# CHAPTER 11

The November 5, 2024 election day would soon be upon the nation, and the Tri-Party was in total disarray. It had no real platform; the economy was a disaster; their social programs, particularly their Medicare for All program, broke the treasury; their fake Russian collusion dossier against President Trumpmeyer was proven to be a total lie; their attempt to impeach the duly elected president turned out to be a farce; and their backing of Antifa, the Boogaloo Bois, and the BLM radicals when the riots broke out, supposedly over the murder of a black man by a Minneapolis policeman, tore the country apart, even though the nation knew the uprisings were politically motivated.

The left also stalled legislation designed to help the unemployed Americans who lost their jobs during the COVID-19 pandemic and it angered the recipients; in their quest for power, the left also refused to fund a border wall designed to stop rapists, drug smugglers, MS-13 gang members, criminals fleeing prosecution in their native countries, and human traffickers from infiltrating the country in great numbers.

But their most insidious action was to allow those millions of illegal aliens into the country with the intent of swelling their party rolls in order to change the United States into a socialistic, one-party nation, even though they knew no socialist country has ever stood the test of time. They were well aware that the socialist governments ruling in China, Russia, Laos, Cuba, and Vietnam are run by dictators and that they are blatant violators of humanities' God-given rights!

On Election Day 2024, Antifa, the Boogaloo Bois, and the radical element of Black Lives Matter reared their ugly heads once again, and the newly sworn in President Ramirez was forbidden by the Posse Comitatus Act to send troops to maintain order and to ensure the safety of the voting public. This did not bode well for Republicans who wanted to exercise their constitutional right to vote.

However, it didn't matter at this point, because the Tri-Party wasn't really running the country anymore. Millions of "We the People" were now calling the shots, and they took things into their own hands at the polling places. This time it would be different when the terrorist groups showed up at polling places across the nation brandishing guns, baseball bats, and chains, still chanting, "No more Trumpmeyer, no more wall, no more USA at all."

The radicals were met by a group of men and women whose own adopted motto mirrored that of Thomas Jefferson, the third American president, and Thomas Paine, an American patriot: "The strongest reason for the people to retain the right to keep and bear arms is, as a last resort, to protect themselves against tyranny in government."

They wore brassards around their left arms depicting the American flag in the background and the symbol of a screaming eagle defending it. Below the eagle's outstretched talons were the letters "AEM"—the acronym for American Eagle Militia.

"Who are you voting for?" the terrorists angrily shouted at each voter. If they answered, "President Ramirez," the terrorists cheered.

But for the first time in four years, American Conservatives were not afraid to go to the polls, and vote they did in unprecedented numbers. When they were asked who they were voting for, they angrily retorted, "It's none of your god-damned business." The terrorists then knew that voter was a Trumpmeyer supporter and they jeered, but that's all they could do.

The remnants of young Antifa thugs, the BLM radicals, and the Boogaloo Bois could only stand idly by at a distance with their weapons, cursing and making threatening but meaningless gestures at the Trumpmeyer voters, but always under the vigilant and daunting eyes of the AEM; their numbers and firepower at every polling station across the nation was awesome. It was grassroots Americans at their finest!

The AEM members, those ordinary everyday Americans, were of every race, color, and creed, and they were there when the polls opened and escorted the voters from their cars to the polling centers and made sure they got safely inside while others stood by, making sure no one damaged their cars. When a citizen finished voting, armed militiamen escorted them back to their cars and waited until they drove safely away. Those actions were taken millions of times on Election Day at thousands of polling places across the nation, and numbered amongst finest hours of American patriots in the history of the United States!

* * *

There were no mail-in ballots, and when the votes were counted, they portrayed the red firestorm that swept the country. The Republicans retook the White House and the House, and retained the Senate. They also won a number of governorships. At Ronald J. Trumpmeyer's swearing-in ceremony as the 47th President of the United States, the Secret Service, US Marshals, and elements of every branch of the US military stood by to ensure his and every attendees' safety.

In spite of the economic disaster that had devastated the country, several million private citizens traveled to Washington, DC to witness the event, including more than a million armed American Eagle Militiamen who were standing by in precise military formations, ready to assist the government forces in case of any emergency. This AEM conglomeration was the largest formation of armed American patriots in the history of the United States, much akin to the patriots who long ago had gathered on the village green with their muskets and defied the most powerful nation on earth: the British Empire.

The AEM's wish and their right to assemble to protect and defend their country and their Constitution against any domestic or foreign oppression are, as a last resort, guaranteed by that bedrock of freedom, the Second Amendment of the

Constitution! That defining amendment gives an American citizen the right to keep and bear arms, and that right is just as important today as it was to the armed citizenry of colonial America more than 244 years ago.

Historians say that at the start of the American Revolution, the first shot fired near the North Bridge in Concord, New Hampshire was the shot heard around the world. When the 2025 swearing-in ceremony of Ronald J. Trumpmeyer was completed, the cheers of more than 200 million Americans was the shout heard around the world, and it fell on the ears of the communist dictators in China, Russia, Cuba, Vietnam, Laos, and Venezuela.

They now know there were three things they could never defeat in this free and democratic nation: the American spirit, the American military, and if necessary as a last resort, an armed American citizenry. That triad was born when that brazen colonist pulled the trigger on his musket at Concord and marked the beginning of the end of the British Empire in North America and around the world. But that trilogy can only be nourished by the strong leadership of presidents like George Washington, Abraham Lincoln, Ronald Reagan, and Donald J. Trumpmeyer! The weak rule of the socialist president, governors, and mayors had left a wake of destruction in America's largest cities and a spate of freshly-dug graves in cemeteries in nearly every state in the union.

They left the country in financial ruin, food prices were still sky high, fossil fuel was scarce, and millions of illegal aliens were left in political limbo. The Second American Civil War was at an end, but pockets of hatred still simmered all across the land and would for generations to come, just as it happened in the aftermath of the American Civil War of 1861–1865.

However, restoring hope and trust in government is a daunting task even for a brash and courageous leader like Ronald J. Trumpmeyer. It is a more difficult challenge than his Making America Great Again campaign had been. The new and arduous task ahead is to reunite America and make it greater than it has ever been before!

* * *

During the ensuing months, two thirds of the Republican-controlled Congress called for an Article V Convention. Under consideration before that lawful body must be: should the validity of the Second Amendment and the Electoral College remain intact, and should the president's term in office remain at the current two four-year terms?

Should the requirement for impeaching a president or a federal judge remain at a simple majority of the House, although that impeachment alone does imply the power to remove a president or a federal judge from office?

Should it remain lawful to remove a president or a federal judge from office following a trial and a vote to convict by two thirds of the Senate?

It should take but one day of debate before the Congress to keep those constitutional mandates intact.

Another proposal before the Article V Convention members must be term limits. Effective with the ratification of three fourths of the Congress, the new 28th Amendment would limit a senator to two six-year terms, and a representative to six two-year terms. The time limits would apply whether you served the full 12 years in the House or Senate or a combination of service in both those bodies. Therefore, the extremely generous retirement benefits the Congress has allotted itself, which is a full pension at age 62 after only five years of service, must be nullified. Thus, any existing service of 20 and 25 years would also be null and void due to term limits.

Congress should contribute to and be eligible for Social Security benefits and Medicare coverage at the same age as the general public. However, the very generous medical benefits they now enjoy would be in effect only while they serve in office.

Should there be severe curtailment of the corrupt lobbyist bloc concerning monetary contributions to politicians and candidates for reelection or those running initially, as well as buying them dinners, paying for their vacations, travel, and lodging expenses? Shouldn't the salaries of these so-called "public servants" be voted on by the merits of their actions as determined by American citizens?

Will a pending Article V Convention ratify these changes the voting public so fervently desires, or will the fake news media, the swampers, and the current corrupt politicians continue to prevail?

Time will tell!

# EPILOGUE

The unethical practices of lobbyists that US senators and representatives so highly cherish is being viewed more and more by the grassroots American public as a form of tyranny. In the United States, we call it lobbying, but in the rest of the world it is called bribery and corruption.

The raises Congress continually bestows upon itself, as well as the lavish travel and medical benefits, the ultra-extravagant retirement system that the Congress so treasures, their abuses of power, and their violations of our constitutional stipulations that go unpunished raises to the level of self-serving dictators. The American taxpayer has absolutely no say in these matters, which is antithetical to a constitutional democracy; thus, the Congress of the United States is autocratic in these self-serving endeavors.

The current Tri-Party members, their supporters, the swampers from both parties, the professional bureaucrats who were not elected and can't be fired, and the other despotic governmental officials in federal law enforcement had better beware of what happened to Benito Mussolini, a radical extremist and former member of the Italian Socialist Party and the National Fascist Party. After the grassroots Italian public had enough of his tyrannical conduct, they executed him by firing squad during the Italian Civil War in 1945.

The majority of the American public is also growing angry and weary of the current insurgents' murder spree, riots, arson, looting, defunding of police departments, rapes, sedition, and the treasonous acts now taking place in the large cities across the nation that are supported by the Tri-Party—the Democratic Party in disguise. Their failure to condemn and loathe the words and actions of a minor group of insurgents, who are intent on destroying our Constitution and our way of life, is an outright case of treason; such behavior marks the initial stages of the tyranny of a rebellious minority struggling to attain absolute parliamentary power. Such insidious treachery can only be met by the vigorous and equally forceful words and, if necessary, the momentous actions of a patriotic American electorate.

Thus, if and when any historic action by the majority becomes necessary, we the people must carefully remind those aforementioned perpetrators of the warning of Thomas Jefferson and Thomas Paine, as their words come echoing ever so loudly to us from across the centuries: "The strongest reason for the people to retain the right to keep and bear arms is, as a last resort, to protect themselves against tyranny in government."

Let us hope and pray that the balance of constitutional powers between our judicial, legislative, and executive branches prevails, and that no such drastic action such as another American Civil War will ever come to pass!